The Practical Executive and Team-Building

ERIC SKOPEC, PH.D.
DAYLE M. SMITH, PH.D.

Series Editor, Arthur H. Bell, Ph.D.

Printed on recyclable paper

NTC Business Books
a division of *NTC Publishing Group* • Lincolnwood, Illinois USA

658.312
S42p

Library of Congress Cataloging-in-Publication Data

Skopec, Eric W., 1946–
    The practical executive and team-building / Eric Skopec, Dayle M.
Smith ; series editor Arthur H. Bell.
      p.   cm.
    Includes bibliographical references and index.
    ISBN 0-8442-2982-2 (alk. paper)
    1. Work groups. I. Smith, Dayle M. II. Title.
HD66.S58   1997
658.3'128—dc20   96-45996
                                              CIP

Published by NTC Business Books, a division of NTC Publishing Group
4255 West Touhy Avenue
Lincolnwood (Chicago), Illinois 60646-1975, U.S.A.
© 1997 by NTC Publishing Group. All rights reserved.
No part of this book may be reproduced, stored in a retrieval system,
or transmitted in any form or by any means,
electronic, mechanical, photocopying, recording or otherwise,
without the prior permission of NTC Publishing Group.
Manufactured in the United States of America.

6 7 8 9 0 VP 9 8 7 6 5 4 3 2 1

Contents

Preface   v

Acknowledgments   vii

Introduction   xi

CHAPTER ONE

Teams in Context   1

CHAPTER TWO

Creating the Team   17

CHAPTER THREE

Leading Teams   31

CHAPTER FOUR

Participating on Teams   43

CHAPTER FIVE

Using Teams Effectively   55

CHAPTER SIX

Problem-Solving with Teams 69

CHAPTER SEVEN

Trouble-Shooting Team Obstacles 87

CHAPTER EIGHT

Technology for Teamwork 101

CHAPTER NINE

Supporting the Team 117

APPENDIX ONE

Problem-Identification Instruments 133

APPENDIX TWO

Team Member Selector 153

APPENDIX THREE

Notes 163

Suggested Readings 167

Index 175

Preface

Most Valuable Players in athletics. Oscar and Emmy winners. Prominent business and political leaders selected for public honors. All these individuals inevitably convey one message when they are asked to speak about their success: they couldn't have done it without the support of their team.

For the past decade, teams have emerged in greater number and greater importance throughout business, industry, government, and not for profit organizations. Drs. Eric Skopec and Dayle Smith have been in the thick of things, helping companies decide when and how to use teams, how to choose team members and leaders, what training to provide for teams, how to evaluate team performance, and how to overcome obstacles encountered along the way. The authors have consulted with organizations in virtually all major industry groups. Their client list reads like a "Who's Who" of firms in aerospace, electronics and microelectronics, finance, retail groups, health care, hospitality, insurance, manufacturing telecommunications, government, and charitable organizations.

In this book, Skopec and Smith share what they've learned from these experiences as well as the most relevant academic research on teams, creativity, and problem solving. The result is a how-to handbook on teams for executives, managers, team leaders and team members—a reliable summary showing how teams can revolutionize business processes in companies large and small. In dozens of company examples, Skopec and Smith tell not only how teams *should* function but also how they *are* working right now in American corporations.

Most important of all, the authors make clear that a work group is not necessarily a work team. These pages explain in interesting detail the business meaning of *e pluribus unum*—out of many individuals, one team.

Arthur H. Bell
McLaren School of Business
University of San Francisco

Acknowledgments

The authors are grateful for the input of hundreds of team members, team leaders, and executives at dozens of business and government organizations. Thanks go especially to teams and team trainers at the U.S. State Department, Santa Fe, Cost Plus World Markets, Global Technologies, Lockheed, Bain & Company, Price-Waterhouse, Paine Webber, Levi-Strauss, Sun Microsystems, Hilton Corporation, Countrywide Credit, American Stores, Charles Schwab, Colonial Williamsburg Foundation, Private Industry Council of Los Angeles, the Central Intelligence Agency, Cushman-Wakefield, Deutsche Telekom, China Resources, Ltd., ANA, TRW, and Marriott Corporation. The authors also learned much from observing and participating in academic teams at Harvard University, University of Southern California, Syracuse University, California State University–Long Beach, University of San Francisco, Old Dominion University, and Georgetown University.

Eric Skopec dedicates this book to his son
Christopher William

Dayle Smith dedicates this book to her daughters
Lauren Elizabeth and Madeleine Alexis

Introduction

Our overriding objective in writing this book is to provide you with the best possible guidance for your work with teams. Here's what you will find as you read the chapters in order. Chapter 1 will put teams in a present-day business context: where they came from, how they have evolved, and, hopefully, where they are headed. Chapter 2 will show you how to create work teams in your organization. Chapter 3 describes the responsibilities and opportunities of team leaders. Chapter 4 treats the interpersonal behaviors of team members. In Chapter 5, you will learn how and when to employ teams. Chapter 6 focuses on proven approaches to structured problem-solving for teams. Chapter 7 shows you how to troubleshoot teams and team processes. Chapter 8 describes new technologies that can enhance team performance. Chapter 9 summarizes the major themes of the book with specific suggestions for supporting and nurturing teams in your organization. Finally, three appendixes conclude the book with a variety of helpful tools. Appendix 1 provides you with a description of useful team instruments. Appendix 2 contains the Team Member Selector test that you can use to build teams made up of complementary personalities. Appendix 3 lists dozens of recent articles and books on aspects of teams and teamwork.

CHAPTER

1

Teams in Context

*We simply cannot afford the luxury of managing
people in the same way as we have in the past.
All managers have had to become more of a
coach and a counsellor, leaders who are
receptive to the notion of empowerment.*[1]

> Stephen Croni
> Group Personnel Director
> Rank Xerox

GM's Delco-Remy plant in Fitzgerald, Georgia, is organized into 25 operations teams
and 5 technical support teams reporting to an
executive team made up of the plant manager
and head supervisors. The operations teams
arrange and monitor their own hours, handle
safety inspections and preventative measures,

repair and maintain their own equipment, recruit new team members, and prepare and administer their own budgets. All quality control in the plant is the responsibility of these teams. Each team member takes his or her turn as team leader.

This bold team approach to managing old problems and seizing new opportunities is the *primary strategy* by which U.S. corporations are striving to succeed. Why? As *Forbes* concluded in its Annual Report on American Industry, "In the 1990s you can go from market dominance to decay in a couple of years. Only the nimble can avoid that fate."

Teams provide that nimbleness. They are at the forefront of American thinking about management. It is probably fair to say that more money has been spent on team-building than on any other innovation in American companies and government organizations. Teams have become a dominant force in business and industry because they are seen as the best means of responding to an extraordinary set of challenges faced by American companies.

WHY TEAMS? WHY NOW?

A broadbrush look at recent history reveals that firms throughout the world are responding to five major challenges. As you will see, the use of teams has been the *common element* among firms that have met the challenges successfully. By understanding these challenges, you will equip yourself with valuable insight and important tools your firm can use to respond.

Globalization

The most visible trend is the evolution of truly global industries. A few decades ago, most industries were dominated by domestic producers. Many imported some raw materials, but most produced and sold their products and services domestically. Foreign sales were thought of as supplementary opportunities.

But that has changed. Since World War II, improvements in transportation and information technology coupled with the lifting of barriers to international trade have promoted the development of global corporations. Today, it is not uncommon for products to be designed in one country, assembled in another country from components manufactured in a variety of locations, and sold in multiple geographic regions. Automobiles are a good example. An icon of American industrial might in the 1950s, today it is virtually impossible to find a car that is a wholly domestic product.

Technological Change

Simultaneously, technological change has generated enormous pressure to "keep up" with competitors and customers. Facilities expected to last decades now become obsolete in a matter of years. Product life cycles may be measured in months. High-tech industries provide countless examples. Here are a couple that stand out.

Just a few years ago, well-meaning and informed observers speculated that the personal computer industry would "settle down" because machines based on 80286 chips provided all the computing power users would need for the foreseeable future. The ink of these pronouncements barely had time to dry as 286-based machines were superseded by those based on 386, 486, and Pentium class chips. The number of transistors per chip as well as processing power measured in millions of instructions per second (MIPS) has increased dramatically with each new generation (see Table 1.1).

The effects of technology are even more pronounced in telecommunications. Distinctions between voice, data, and video transmission are rapidly becoming incidental, and few companies can count on secure niches. Telephone companies have promoted "dial tone video" in their efforts to enter the "infotainment" industry, but most have faltered. Federal Communications Commission procedures require companies to commit to a particular technology as part of their application, but in many cases the technology is obsolete before construction begins—in extreme cases before the application was even approved!

TABLE 1.1
PROCESSOR POWER

Year	State-of-the-Art Chip	Number of Transistors	MIPS
1978	8086	29,000	less than 1
1982	80286	134,000	1–2
1985	80386	275,000	6–12
1989	80486	1,200,000	20–40
1993	Pentium	3,200,000	100–200
1995	P6	5,500,000	300+

Competition and Rivalry

With globalization and technological change have come dramatic increases in the scope, level, and location of one's competitors. Firms that were once protected by national boundaries or proprietary technologies have suddenly found themselves in a radically changed competitive environment. Characterized by "hypercompetition," this is an environment of intense pressure, allowing flexible, aggressive, innovative competitors to move into new markets easily and destroy the advantages of large, established firms. A company's competitors are just as likely to be around the world as around the corner.

Workforce Diversity

A few decades ago, the American workforce was predominantly white and male. Today, in contrast, white males are the slowest growing segment of the population, and the composition of the workforce is changing as a result. Dramatic differences in birth rates have increased the percentage of "minority" workers while equal opportunity legislation has opened professional roles previously closed. Changing societal mores have increased the number of women seeking full-time employment, and they have benefited from efforts to prevent discrimination as well. Finally, evolving immigration patterns have fundamentally altered the composition of the workforce. Today, one person of five in major cities was born outside the United States, and all indicators point to continued growth of foreign-born workers.

These waves of change have brought together myriad cultures, expectations, and needs that cannot be overlooked. Employment practices that are the norm for some groups are barely acceptable to others and profoundly offensive to still others.

Changing Customer Expectations

Finally, customer expectations have changed dramatically. Today's companies serve consumers from a variety of cultures, and features that once commanded high prices are accepted as commonplace today. Moreover, we have learned some important things about satisfying customers. Quality can only be defined in terms of the customer's expectations, and customers' expectations are constantly changing. Innovations in one industry create expectations that "generalize" to all: customers who can get lunch in five minutes or less at a "fast food" restaurant are seldom willing to wait much longer for a new telephone or computer.

SUCCESSFUL ORGANIZATIONAL RESPONSES

While the challenges are extraordinary by almost any standard, innovative companies have responded in ways designed to assure their roles as world leaders. More than two thirds of *Fortune* 1000 companies use teams and every one of the finalists in a recent *Industry Week* search for the best manufacturing plants employs cross-functional teams for special projects. Eight initiatives are responsible for many team applications, all of which are essential to most efforts to respond to the changing business environment.

Empowerment

Traditionally, employees on the front line had little authority. Most were expected to follow directions and work according to accepted procedures with little variation. Day in and day out, employees witnessed problems that they were powerless to correct. Something as simple as repairing a malfunctioning machine required a supervisor's approval, while variations in accepted procedures called for even more elaborate approvals, sometimes three or more levels removed from the particular activity.

Today, innovative companies have replaced arcane command-and-control structures with self-directed work teams, which are given broad discretion in performing their tasks and in making changes in materials, methods, machines, and manpower. Of course, these teams are accountable for their performance and often rewarded for exercising initiative.

When implemented properly, dramatic improvements in company performance have been often associated with self-directed work teams. For example, American Express cut out three layers of hierarchy when it developed self-managed teams, and all types of customer inquiries now are handled with a single call. Quick (and less costly) resolution is the norm.

Total Quality Management

Total quality management is a fundamental rethinking of product and service priorities. It can be understood best in a historical context. The ability to produce large quantities of standardized goods at relatively cheap prices is an enduring legacy of the industrial revolution. World War II accentuated the emphasis on volume production, and following the war, there was so much pent-up demand for consumer goods that customers were satisfied with merely serviceable products.

The emphasis on volume production began to change in the early 1950s. Japanese companies with modern facilities discovered that they could capture markets by offering higher quality products at competitive prices. As they began to dominate the automotive and consumer electronics industries, companies worldwide were forced to respond and the total quality movement was born.

Teams are essential components of quality programs for two reasons. First, people are more likely to support initiatives in which they have played a significant role. This bit of psychology benefits corporations because employee involvement leads to increased commitment to quality management.

Second, teams provide a convenient means of dealing with problems arising from organizational boundaries. Most companies are organized into divisions, departments, and subdepartments reflecting specific areas of competence. Finance, marketing, research and development, engineering, and operations are common examples. While these units are convenient ways of organizing a firm, problems affecting customers are not so easily partitioned. Operations must be capable of delivering what sales promises and specialized problems may require coordination of four, five, or even more separate units. Teams with members representing each of the departments involved are the most effective means of addressing issues that span organizational boundaries. Today, many companies realize that some problems extend beyond their corporate borders. In response, they have deployed teams that include suppliers, shippers, distributors, and customers as well as members of their own departments.

Customer Response Teams

Customer response teams have reshaped many organizations, improving customer satisfaction, winning new orders, and eliminating many of the hassles encountered in dealing with complaints. Understanding their importance calls for a backward look at traditional systems.

Traditionally, the customer has direct contact only with the salesperson. As long as the customer is satisfied with a generic product or service and the system was running properly, things ran pretty smoothly. However, seemingly endless approvals were required if the customer requested even minor modifications in the standard product or service. A change in delivery schedule required approvals from purchasing, manufacturing, and shipping. Each department had the authority to say "no," but none had the authority to approve the customer request. Worse yet, customer requests often spent more time being passed from department to department than actually being processed. One organization found that customer requests routinely requiring six weeks to process actually involved no more than three hours of "real" work.

Today, organizations employing customer response teams have minimized the paper chase. Cross-functional teams have the knowledge and authority to speak for each department and respond to most requests on the spot. Unusual requests may require team members to place a call or two, but even they are handled quickly and efficiently. And, both companies and customers have benefited from the change.

Design Teams

Market conditions often make it desirable to bring new products to market rapidly and efficiently. Traditional approaches compromised both objectives and many companies have found design teams to be an attractive alternative.

In a traditional system, products are designed in a sequential manner by independent departments. Here is how it often works. The Marketing Department develops a product concept and does some initial market testing. The product concept is then passed to Sales for its approval before the concept is sent to Research and Development. R&D creates and tests one or more prototypes before the concept is forwarded to Process Engineering, which develops the manufacturing process. Eventually, the finished design is sent to Purchasing, which must buy raw materials or components and then on to Manufacturing, which produces the finished product. Other departments such as Shipping may get time to review the concept as well, and any of the departments involved may object to one or more features. Even minor problems "down the line" may force the product back to the drawing board and months of work may be undone by design changes. It is not uncommon for a single product to be redesigned a dozen times or more, and change orders float through the system like blowing snow on a windy day.

Faced with growing competition, many companies have replaced traditional processes with design teams. Using an approach known as "concurrent engineering" or "simultaneous design," these companies assemble teams composed of representatives from all the affected departments. These teams are authorized to make all key decisions and the simultaneous input insures that minor problems don't require major changes later on. Months, sometimes years, are shaved off the development process.

Much of Chrysler's revitalization is due to dramatically revamping its new-model development process using "platform teams." Each platform team consists of members from engineering, design, finance, purchasing, and marketing. The team is responsible for the car's design from beginning to end, and has broad decision-making power, and is held accountable for the success or failure of the design. Teams coordinate their designs with manufacturing so that the models are easier to build and consult regularly with purchasing agents regarding parts quality. In one case, Chrysler purchasing agents elected to pay 30 percent more for a better part because the engineer on the platform team believed the added cost would be offset by the time saved during assembly. Ford and General Motors have followed suit in using design teams to speed products to market.

New Venture Teams

Launching a new business is a daunting task because so many distinct issues need to be considered at one time. Topics that must be addressed include: potential market size and characteristics; primary suppliers and vendors; probable competitor reactions to the new company; appropriate product, manufacturing, and service technology; sources and costs of start-up financing; organizational structures and incorporation requirements; employee hiring, training, and management; and marketing, advertising, and sales strategies.

New venture teams may be as small as three people or as large as fifteen or more but all of the necessary areas of expertise are represented. And, when the new venture is an outgrowth of an existing company, one member is responsible for maintaining a smooth interface with the parent company. Dow, General Mills, Westinghouse, General Electric, and Monsanto among others have used new venture teams with great success.

Reengineering

Reengineering is among the most recent responses to competitive challenges. It originates with efforts to apply information technologies to manufacturing processes and an understanding of why some efforts failed. Beginning in the 1950s, increasing numbers of companies began computerizing their core processes. In spite of substantial investments, many did not achieve anticipated improvements. Professionals studying the problem eventually discovered its root cause: in adopting computers, many companies had merely automated inefficient systems. They had, in effect, "paved over cow paths" without fundamentally improving operations.

Recognizing that dramatic gains in efficiency require fundamental redesign, information systems professionals and consultants began to develop ways of redesigning corporate processes to support and reflect changes in technology. By the time the reengineering movement gained widespread public attention in the early 1990s, its basic principles including the use of teams, were well established.

Project Teams and Task Forces

Rigid compartmentalization is one of the hallmarks of the industrial revolution. Dividing each work process into even smaller components and assigning responsibility for each to a specific division, department, or subdepartment makes it possible to exercise precise control over each step in a complex process.

Today, however, many organizations are finding that compartmentalization limits their ability to respond to situations that span departmental boundaries. For example, quality problems may involve the purchasing, receiving, engineering, manufacturing, and human resources departments. Similarly, introducing a new product may require the attention of Marketing, Sales, Engineering, Purchasing, Manufacturing, and even Finance. Many organizations have found that task forces and project teams are the best ways to cope with situations that involve several departments.

Both task forces and project teams are separate, largely self-sufficient work groups. Generally, they are formed to oversee the completion of a specific, one-time activity with a finite life expectancy in a situation where the normal organization is not equipped to achieve the same results in addition to regular duties. Typical projects include setting up a new technological process, bringing out a new product, starting up a new venture, consummating a merger with another company, seeing through the completion of a government contract, and supervising the construction of a new plant. Some may last a few weeks or months, but others may require a year or more. Members range from senior-level executives working on projects with broad strategic implications to front-line employees engaged in more limited exercises.

Whole-Enterprise Perspectives

Finally, teams and teamwork have begun to transform the role of senior management. Traditionally, only the board of directors and president or chief executive officer and board of directors were responsible for the health of the organization as a whole. Other executives, even the most senior, focused attention on the performance of their own units. In single business organizations, senior managers were drawn from specific functions and expected to represent their interests.

Today, the pattern is changing, slowly but perceptibly, as all senior managers are expected to use their knowledge and expertise on behalf of the firm as a whole. They may even be expected to sacrifice the interests of their department in favor of the general good.

The tone of senior management meetings in innovative organizations has changed significantly as a result of this trend. Today the defensiveness and posturing that once characterized senior management meetings is less common, and generally considered to be less acceptable. Arguments and disagreements remain, but they start from a different premise. Rather than asking, "How will this affect my department?" senior managers have begun asking, "How will this affect the firm as a whole?"

THE BLUE CHIP TEAM

The eight initiatives above pervade American business and industry. As a result, countless teams are at work every day, but their track records are mixed. Many have been remarkably successful, overcoming challenges that threatened the very survival of their companies and producing innovations that have changed the face of business and society. Others have been moderately successful; some teams have merely "broken even"; and, sadly, a handful have been dramatic failures.

Only a few qualify as "Blue Chip Teams"—those that achieve their missions without needlessly consuming valuable resources and often do far more than was expected of them.

Blue Chip status is a lofty ideal to which every team should aspire. A quick look at the characteristics of Blue Chip Teams will help to point us in the right direction.

Identity

The extent to which members identify with the team is the most noticeable characteristic of blue chip teams. Even though members are typically drawn from separate departments, they quickly come to identify with the team and their original assignment becomes a secondary or incidental factor. One team member described her transition in the following words:

> At first, I thought of myself as the finance department representative on the team. However, once we really got going, I realized that I was a member of the team, first and foremost, and my original work in finance was just a way of getting ready for the team project.

Achieving this degree of identification with a team is as important as it is uncommon. Once established, however, identification with the team is a source of pride and motivation. Moreover, such pride translates into outstanding performance. It is common to hear blue chip team members explain extraordinary achievements by saying that "I couldn't let my team down."

Mission

Second only to identification, blue chip team members share an extraordinary sense of mission. Collectively, they see their project as much of a quest or destiny as a job. When asked to describe their project, most are likely to begin by talking about the project's goal. Ask them why they are doing it and most will talk about the jobs that will be created or saved and about the people whose lives will be affected. In short, blue chip team members see their work in terms of overriding social objectives and their ability to contribute to the well-being of their colleagues and customers.

Great Expectations

The third defining characteristic of a blue chip team is the great expectations of its members. As a group, they not only expect to get the job done, they expect to do it in a grand style. Few think about modest improvements in efficiency of 5%, 10%, or even 15%. Instead, they aim for dramatic improvements—doubling, tripling, or even quadrupling measures of performance.

Of course, not all blue chip teams fulfill their expectations. The important thing is what they aim for. And, these expectations translate into superior performance because team members are not satisfied until they reach lofty heights.

Commonly Accepted Procedures

The fourth characteristic of blue chip teams is a bit of a curiosity. Research and experience indicate that certain procedures are more likely to produce better results than others. The curious thing is that many blue chip teams develop procedures that are inconsistent with what experts might recommend. Many deviate in a few particulars while others literally write their own rule books.

In spite of the diversity of procedures, one thing stands out: blue chip team members know what the procedures are and accept them as their own. They know what issues will be addressed by the team, what procedures will be used, and how any conflicts will be resolved. As a result, we have come to believe that common understanding and acceptance of procedures is more important than outside recommendations.

Feedback

Finally, blue chip team members commonly review team performance and provide feedback to one another and the team as a whole. They congratulate themselves on their successes and treat failures as opportunities for improvement. Individual members actively seek feedback, accept it without defensiveness, and provide feedback to others in objective, nonthreatening ways.

Feedback is essential because it permits teams to engage in double-loop problem solving. Single-loop approaches deal with an immediate problem, but they don't touch the underlying causes. Problems come back to haunt one again and again. In contrast, double-loop approaches solve the immediate problem and develop procedures that prevent it from becoming a problem again. For example, a personal conflict between two team members can be devastating. A single-loop approach merely silences the argument and gets the team back to work while underlying issues remain unresolved. In contrast, double-loop strategies solve the immediate problem and deal with the underlying issues through effective feedback. As a result, the team can get back to work without standing guard over the interaction between the two members.

Team-Building

The term *team-building* is used to describe efforts to create teams capable of outstanding achievements. Here's how we define it: *Team-building is a structured series of activities designed to improve the performance of a team.* Typical activities include reviewing individual members' personality profiles, analysis of the group's composite profile, cognitive simulations such as group "survival" exercises, role playing "games," physical tests like rock climbing, and cooperative problem-solving sessions. The objective is to improve communication between members, enhance coordination and cooperation, prepare the group for special projects, and develop skills needed to accomplish specific tasks.

2

Creating the Team

*The 10,000 runners in the New York City
marathon race have a common goal or purpose.
However, they are not a team. They are, in fact,
in competition with each other. Teamwork
requires interdependence—the working together
of a group of people with a shared objective.[1]*

William Fox
Division Manager
Bell Communications Research

Quad Graphics specializes in printing high-quality magazines. The company has virtually no hierarchies of management below the CEO level. Day-to-day operations, new product and service development, purchasing, personnel functions, and most salary decisions are handled by teams. But at Quad Graphics, the emphasis is not only on what teams do, but what they *are* . . . and how they can emerge, serve, and evolve. Employees care so much about their teams, in fact, that they willingly train and cross-train in team skills for four hours each week *on their own time*. This use of personal time in team development is considered by many Quad Graphics employees their best investment for future financial and professional security. And with good reason: employees own 40 percent of the company. They organize into teams not because they were told to do so, but because they know they can grow *their company* best through flexible teamwork.[2]

Creating effective work teams, like those at Quad Graphics, isn't a matter of luck or some executive's bright idea for this week's new form of organization. Too many corporate leaders have tried to create teams in their organizations by mandate. This approach to team creation is termed the "Savior syndrome" by Carl Harshman and Steven Phillips in *Teaming Up*.[3] Just as companies often seek a new CEO as a savior for company ills, so they now may try to convert abruptly to team-based work with the hope that it will revolutionize company processes and maximize profits.

It doesn't.

THINKING ABOUT WORK IN NEW WAYS

Creating effective teams requires what Thomas Kuhn calls a *paradigm shift* in how work itself is conceptualized in the company.[4] Consider eight ways in which teamwork differs from traditional work:

1. In the team, leadership is shared; even a designated "group leader" is more a facilitator or coach than a boss. In traditional work, leadership (and resulting power) is centralized in a hierarchy of supervisors, managers, and executives, whereas in a team, it is decentralized.

2. Teams themselves decide upon tasks and schedules. In traditional work, these decisions are made for workers by management.

3. Teams are generally responsible for completing an entire job. Traditional workers complete only a portion of the job before handing it over to others.

4. Team members receive training and practice in interpersonal skills as well as technical skills. Traditional workers tend to receive training only in technical skills.

5. Team members are paid for what they can do (their skills) and their productivity. Traditional workers are usually paid for their time.

6. Team members develop trust and caring for one another, even though they may individually come from quite different functions in the organization (e.g., accounting and engineering). Traditional workers often develop an "us against them" attitude toward workers in other company divisions.

7. In an effective team, quality improvement measures are developed by the team itself. In traditional work, quality control inspections and sanctions are imposed upon workers by supervisors and managers.

8. Teams meet regularly to set goals, diagnose and resolve problems, and review and report progress. Traditional workers meet rarely with one another, and then usually for the sole purpose of receiving information.

What happens when these crucial differences are not understood throughout the organization? Managers will tend to withhold the information the team needs to succeed. Supervisors may disparage the ability of lower-level workers to find solutions that have eluded management. And workers themselves may come to look upon teamwork as a time-wasting activity.

Preparing the Organization

Expressions of concern or frustration are not indications that team-based work is wrong for the organization. Instead, they signal that the organization has not properly prepared itself for the effective use teams. The company leadership must talk *often* with employees about the new values that underlie a team-based approach to work.

Company leadership must demonstrate in their behaviors and new attitudes:

- Role 1: To make powerful employees, not to gather power to oneself.

- Role 2: To teach and counsel more than criticize and command.

- Role 3: To welcome positive change, not to glorify the status quo.

- Role 4: To reward and motivate much more often than to punish and discourage.

Company reward systems as well must be oriented toward team work, not just individual achievement. Information about work standards and processes must be available. Employees should know that the team-based approach to work has an impressive and time-tested track record. According to the Work in America Institute, teams have been a primary form of internal organization at hundreds of successful companies, including GE since 1985, Procter and Gamble since 1962, Ford since 1982, Boeing since 1987, and Cummins Engine since 1973.[5]

The broad organizational learning that takes place through employee participation in teams should be highlighted by company leadership as a "must-have" to succeed in rapidly changing markets and industries. Members of teams, in the words of Glenn M. Parker, architect of the team system at Merck, Johnson & Johnson, and 3M, "are more easily able to develop new technical and professional skills, learn more about other disciplines, and learn how to work with people who have different team-player styles and cultural backgrounds than those lacking team experience."[6]

In organizations that have prepared to introduce teams, the positive response from employees has been overwhelming. *Training* magazine recently surveyed employees from team-based companies across industries, with the following results:[7]

- Ninety percent said that teams had improved the quality of services and products.

- Eighty-five percent said that customer service had improved as a result of teams.

- Eighty-one percent agreed that teams had improved productivity.

- Eighty percent credited teams with contributing to increased profits.

- Seventy-six percent said that morale had improved as a direct result of team organization.

Preparing the Individual

If individuals are chosen randomly for their first team experience, the result may be more heat than light from the team in the form of complaints, arguments, and general antagonism. An underwriter for a major New England insurance company recalls her "baptism by fire," as she calls it, into the team approach to work:

I was used to working in a rather traditional environment—most hours spent working alone at my desk, with a few hours each week devoted to informational meetings led by my manager. Shortly after the company hired a new CEO, I received a memo telling me that I was now empowered as a member of a new work team, comprised of 11 other employees from various units in the company. The memo went on to instruct our team to meet at least 4 hours a day, to develop agendas for improvements in loan processing, and to implement the best of those agendas as pilot tests.

Frankly, we were floored. Our meetings were chaotic, with each of us struggling to make sense out of what we were supposed to do and how we would be evaluated (or punished!) for doing it. Our daily meetings quickly broke down into quibbling, lectures on pet peeves and private agendas, or discouraged silence. We were all waiting for a traditional manager to come in, set the agenda, and distribute tasks.[8]

With the help of a facilitator, this team eventually got on track. But the individuals involved no doubt wish they had been prepared for participation.

Education

Al Davis, general manager of the Oakland Raiders, tells new members of his team "not to treat problems as special. Treat them as normal."[9] Team members in business organizations, too, should be counseled to expect disagreement, objections, and a certain degree of interpersonal strife as signs that the team is working its way forward, not falling apart. *Knowing* that this stage is a typical part of the evolution of an effective team helps team members maintain morale and optimism for the future of the team.

Selection

The Team Member Selector instrument contained in Appendix 2 describes eight common personality types in business organizations: the Member, the Self, the Planner, the Juggler, the Thinker, the Feeler, the Researcher, and the Closer. The specific uses of these personality inventories for building strong, multidimensional work teams are discussed later in this chapter. For now, it is enough to make the main point about personality variation among workers: the personality types on a team should complement one another.

Lacking complementary members, a team can quickly strangle on its own best qualities. Smaller organizations are particularly vulnerable to these single-type teams. Especially if hiring has been almost exclusively in the hands of a few company leaders, the company over a period of time may come to be populated almost exclusively by one or two personality types. This is the well-known halo effect in hiring, in which a manager unthinkingly hires his or her clone over and over. These candidates seem right for the job and appear to fit the organization—precisely because they exhibit the qualities the boss most approves.

Flexibility of Roles

The role assumed by a given team member is not identical to the member's personality type, although roles and personality types are generally harmonious rather than in conflict. Here is a spectrum of roles necessary for the typical work team:

- The Promoter: This person informs and persuades stakeholders regarding the work of the team.

- The Organizer: This person maintains schedules and budgets and, in general, serves to keep other team members "on the same page."

- The Inspector: This quality-control agent pays careful attention to the production of the team and reports to members on their work as well as on the reliability of their sources of information.

- The Concluder: This person moves the team toward consensus judgments, stages of completion, and final sign-offs.

- The Innovator: This team member brings fresh ideas and insights to the work of the team.

- The Specialist: This person makes sure the team is up to date on technological, marketing, or other information relevant to its work.

- The Implementer: This team member views the work of the team during development and upon project completion according to how it can be put to use in the real world.

These are approximately the roles IBM has used since 1980 in shaping effective teams. No employee is "stuck" in a single role for his or her career, although workers have naturally tended to acquire reputations for their strong skills in one or two roles. By consciously switching roles or developing new roles from time to time, employees at IBM learn to appreciate the motives, perspective, and skills of each role represented on the team. Overall team performance is thus strengthened.

Variety among team members can also be achieved by drawing from different functional areas within the company. At Conagra,

Inc., for example, a highly successful corporate team was assembled from traditionally separate spheres of research, finance, planning, operations, and marketing. G.B. Vernon, vice-president of the company, describes the formation of this team:

> We are a very decentralized company. However, a member of one operating division saw a corporate-wide selling opportunity, pulled together executives from seven of our other businesses, and developed a "corporate sales" concept which led to one of the largest single sales and one of the strongest customer relationships we have.[10]

In the best of all worlds, teams achieve maximum variety of skills and insights when their members differ in personality type from one another, assume compatible and complementary roles, and come from different functional areas within the organization.

Inclusiveness

One boundary enforced by traditional business thinking is the line separating those "inside" the company from those "outside." For most of this century, American corporations have played corporate policy and product development close to the vest, showing suppliers and customers only the finished product when it is ready for sale. Some of these outsiders who had ideas for product or process improvements were told explicitly, "It's none of your business."

Of course, it *is* the business of customers and vendors to want the best product at the best price. With the advent of teams, company doors have been opened to the new ideas and perspectives by former "outsiders." It occurred to teams that the insights and ideas that mattered most—those of the customer—had been foolishly excluded from consideration. In the early 1990s, Motorola was among the first major corporations to repair this oversight. Leaders at Motorola insisted that "members of a true cross-functional team should consist of all levels: management, operators, and technicians, and members from different organizations, including vendors and customers."[11]

These former outsiders can play a full role, with all rights and privileges, on company teams. Or they can influence the work of the team in less formal ways by making presentations, hosting on-site meetings, and providing information about emerging wants and needs. Sun Microsystems, for example, regularly sends its managers and technicians to the facilities of its customers to learn first-hand about market conditions, needs, and directions. Although these customers are not decision-makers in the traditional sense on Sun's various workteams, they nevertheless exert significant influence. As Max DePree, former chairman and CEO of Herman Miller, Inc., has written, "Having a say differs from having a vote."[12]

The Value of Diversity

This suggestion is not a plea for social justice or equal opportunity, although it could be presented in those terms. It is based, instead, on the opportunity for strategic business advantage for companies intending to succeed in a world of changing demographics.

Consider current and near-term realities of the American workplace:

- Women now hold more than 40 percent of all administrative and managerial positions.

- More than half of all new entrants into the labor force in the next five years will come from minority populations.

- As people live longer, they work longer. By 2010, twenty percent of the population will be 62 years or older, according to Department of Labor statistics. As Social Security and other pensions raise their age limits for benefits, we can expect more senior citizens to remain in the workplace, especially for the health benefits it provides.

These facts alone do not mean that work teams will be more diverse in the future. But recent research demonstrates that companies who avoid diversity on their teams are missing a business opportunity. According to researchers Richard Guzzo and Eduardo Salas, companies are seeing "a shift away from viewing diversity as primarily a social issue to viewing it as a strategic business imperative."[13]

Guzzo and Salas found that at Digital Equipment Corporation "top management reports that managing diversity effectively leads to such consequences as a solid reputation as one of the best places to work, an empowered work force, greater innovation, increased productivity, and a competitive advantage in global competition."[14] It stands to reason that a company hoping to develop products or services for Latin America might well include Hispanic workers on its decision-making teams. Similarly, a firm intending to sell to more than half of the U.S. population would do well to welcome gender diversity to its teams.

PepsiCo's recent Snapple debacle in Japan makes the point. Snapple is an ice-tea product with fruit additives; tiny pieces of fruit, in fact, can be seen floating in the product. The dramatic success of Snapple in the United States and Europe bouyed PepsiCo's hopes that it would prove immensely successful in the tea-loving society of Japan. In spite of PepsiCo's best marketing efforts in Japan, the product failed miserably and had to be withdrawn. Japanese executive Ko Horiuchi explains: "PepsiCo obviously didn't understand that we Japanese like fresh tea, not bottled tea. And we hate the idea of little pieces of anything floating in our tea."[15] Had PepsiCo included more diverse viewpoints on its decision-making teams in the Snapple case, the company might have avoided an expensive misstep.

CHARACTERISTICS OF EFFECTIVE TEAMS

You can determine the health of any team by looking for seven indicators:

- Buy-in: Team members share a clear perception of their purpose and commit to that purpose as "our" goal.

- Tolerance for disagreement: Team members handle differences of opinion as a stimulating opportunity for testing and refining their work. They listen well. They can attack positions without attacking people.

- Comfort: Team members are relaxed with one another. They trust the intentions and integrity of fellow team members. They enjoy working together.

- Shared leadership: Even when the company has designated a specific team leader, the team allows de facto leadership to pass from member to member, depending upon the obstacles and tasks at hand for the team. Every member knows he or she can rise to leadership.

- Diversity: Whether differentiated by personality types, roles, culture, or other factors, the members of the team recognize and respect their mutual diversity.

- Reality checks: The team is not self-deceived regarding the quality of its work. Members assess team goals and progress in constructive ways that motivate the pursuit of excellence.

- Consensus-seeking: The team strives for, but does not insist upon, the support of all members for team decisions.

When one or more of these indicators of team effectiveness is missing, it's time for trouble-shooting (see Chapter 7).

Stages of Team Development

Thirty years ago, B.W. Tuckman set forth a four-part scenario for team development: forming, storming, norming, and performing.[16] Earlier in this chapter we have discussed the conditions, organizational and individual, under which effective teams *form*. Tuckman compared this stage to human infancy. Team members are still deeply dependent upon the managers who selected them for the team or the appointed team leader. They look for orientation and direction in virtually all matters: when and where to meet, how to prepare for the meeting, and how to conduct oneself as a team member.

With growing confidence, the infant team enters its "terrible twos," the *storming* stage. Team members indicate by their words, actions, and nonverbal cues their impatience with group processes, their displeasure with the group leader, and their mutual irritation with one another.

At times, a group leader may be so forceful or persuasive a personality as to prevent expressions of storming from surfacing. Team members in these circumstances may play "good boy" or "good girl" at team meetings, only to grouse behind the leader's back or passively resist assigned tasks. Tuckman suggests that teams, like growing children, need to express feelings of rebellion and aggression. By identifying with these expressions instead of forbidding them, the team leader can make a natural transition to team participant and peer from a former position as "parent" or judge.

The experience of one new team leader at a recent American Stores meeting shows how storming, like the terrible twos, can be "just a stage," though a necessary one:

> I think of myself as a relatively easy-going, likable person. That is why I was surprised—shocked, really—to have the team I was leading turn against me at our third meeting. The first two meetings had gone smoothly. Members seemed pleased to be selected for the team and with my leadership style. There was a lot of laughter at these meetings. It all changed to complaints, however, when I passed out work assignments at our third meeting.
>
> My first impulse was to pull rank and tell them to shape up. But I resisted my own frustration and anger long enough to ask the team one question: "What do you think we should do to achieve our goals?" That meeting lasted more than two hours, during which every member had the chance to blow off steam as well as contribute to some tentative planning. Team members who had been at each other's throats seemed to reach a truce toward the end of the meeting. As we left the room, we all had the feeling we

had gone through—and survived—the first argument after the honeymoon. We all felt real, and we knew we could work together.[17]

Storming, of course, isn't over for most teams in a meeting or two. The circumstances, members, tasks, goals, and accompanying pressures all influence how long a team must storm before maturing to its next stage. The only thing worse than going through this phase is *not* going through it by avoiding or suppressing it.

Norming, according to Tuckman, is the third stage in team development. In many ways, this stage is comparable to the socialization or "playmate" stage of childhood development. Team members develop an unwritten but nonetheless binding team culture that governs how members relate to one another, what actions are legal or taboo, and what sanctions are meted out to those who violate the mores of the team culture. Team members gradually give up competitive squabbles and contests for individual attention. Trust and cooperation begin to emerge. Team members feel supported, protected, and respected by one another. The team is nearing the point where it can begin life on its own.

Performing, the last of Tuckman's stages, is comparable to adulthood. The team has achieved good interpersonal working relations and is now ready to define, investigate, and resolve significant problems. Lacking these tasks, in fact, the team will probably wither or, just as often, return to the earlier stages of storming and norming. The passion of the team, in other words, lies in its challenges. Wise corporate leaders help talented teams thrive by turning them loose on the thorniest and most crucial obstacles facing the company. Team members will feel pride in their mutual association to the extent that together they have faced and overcome substantial problems.

No corporate leader should expect teams to neatly pass through Tuckman's four stages without considerable backtracking and repetition. Some management experts, in fact, observe teams going through all of Tuckman's stages at each major stage of development. The period of norming, in other words, includes its own miniature dramas of forming, storming, and so forth.

Team leaders and team members come to understand that change and evolution are a normal part of the team experience. Leaders responsible for teams can redefine themselves, in fact, as managers who *anticipate* change and help team members respond to it productively.

Team-Building Tips

1. Teams will succeed only in organizations who prepare for their success.

2. Individuals should be placed on teams with an eye toward their personality qualities and role abilities.

3. A strong team is made up of diverse members who understand and respect their differences.

4. Teams mature by passing through stages of forming, storming, norming, and performing.

CHAPTER

3

Leading Teams

Lead by example. And the example we wanted was a belief that everyone at every level can contribute, everyone had to challenge everything, everyone had to take more risks, and everyone had to learn new things.[1]

> Sarah Nolan
> President
> Amex Life Assurance

Dallas-based DePalma Hotel Corp. manages fifteen hotels nationwide. The firm keeps its edge over competitors by spotting problems quickly, resolving them in cost-effective ways, and constantly looking for ways to improve services to their clients and hotel guests. This work is the day-to-day business of self-directed teams at DePalma. Managers from food service, sales, housekeeping, and customer service form teams that are accountable to top management, but have no designated leaders. On these teams, says CEO Joseph DePalma, "no one is boss. . . . It's a meeting where people come to look forward to participating instead of coming just to listen to the general manager."[2]

LEADERSHIP STYLES TODAY

The leadership paradox—that leading often means giving up power rather than accumulating it—lies at the heart of managing teams for maximum impact in the organization of the future.

In truth, most teams now active in American corporations are not truly self-directed. Instead, they are *functional* teams assembled by a leader, who runs most meetings and sets (or at least approves) most agenda items and decisions. The leadership skills required for this kind of team management are quite traditional. They seek to:

- Maintain control
- Focus and direct member activities
- Accept responsibility for final decisions
- Set and enforce work and quality standards
- Distribute rewards and sanctions according to member performance
- Motivate team members

For many business situations and purposes, this set of leadership skills is well-suited, at least for attaining short-term organizational goals.

It may fail, however, to serve organizations well in the longer term. Traditional leadership approaches to team management exercise the talents of the leader but do little to encourage independent thinking, innovation, and accountability among team members.

Delegated Leadership

A small step toward less directive leadership involves the delegation of limited team leadership or of selected leadership tasks to team members. In this leadership style, the team is hardly self-directed, of course, The leader is still pulling most of the strings under the guise of giving team members a chance to perform as designated leaders-for-a-day.

Let's say, for example, that a leader asks team members John, Alice, Ruth, and Bill to each serve in turn as meeting leaders for weekly team meetings. To some extent, this option does serve to develop these individuals' leadership skills. But the whole arrangement may come to look and feel like a training exercise— preparing *for* independent initiative rather than practicing it. A lockstep rotation of meeting leaders may also tend to defuse team action agenda items. What seemed important in John's meeting may not be important when Alice, Ruth, or Bill take their turns.

Elected Leadership

A supervisor can turn the selection of leaders over to the team itself. This option certainly empowers team members and underlines their responsibility for independent problem-solving. Interpersonal relations on the team, however, must be sufficiently developed for consensus selection of leaders. Close votes, with a significant minority left grumbling on the sidelines, can sabotage any elected leader's efforts. In addition, there is no guarantee that a team will select the right leader. This undesirable result is all the more likely if team members have no training or experience in team leadership. Old leadership styles may crop up not because they are preferred by the team but because they are familiar.

Shared Leadership

In this leadership approach, the nature of leadership itself undergoes a marked transformation. From the supervisor's point of view, shared leadership means redefining the leader's role in five ways:

- The old leader displays greater knowledge, experience, and wisdom in decision-making than that possessed by team members. The new leader shows others how knowledge, experience, and skill in decision-making can be acquired.

- The old leader tells team members what to do. The new leader participates in deciding with team members what courses of action to take.

- The old leader talks most of the time. The new leader listens most of the time.

- The old leader discourages risk-taking and punishes missteps on the part of team members. The new leader encourages team initiative and accepts risk and occasional failure as part of the learning curve.

- The old leader has a relatively low opinion of the intelligence, motivation, and trustworthiness of team members. The new leader respects team members and values their contributions.

This approach to leadership resolves the problem of "talent divorce," in which one particularly skilled individual (the supervisor) is summarily excluded from team processes. Empowerment of the team by the supervisor, in other words, does not have to mean walking out of the meeting room and hoping for the best. It does mean climbing down from the traditional leadership pedestal.

Once "in the trenches" with the rest of the team, the supervisor exerts *developmental leadership* by three strategies:

1. The supervisor *gets to know* team members and lets himself or herself be known. All team successes will depend directly upon the degree of interpersonal trust shared by team members. The supervisor can begin to build that trust by modeling sincere interest in others.

2. The supervisor *raises process questions* without dictating answers. In early meetings, the supervisor can ask the team such questions as:

- What do you think is our purpose as a team?

- What are our individual roles?
- What norms can we agree upon for our discussions? [For example, we can agree to welcome divergent opinions and seek consensus whenever possible.]

3. The supervisor interprets organizational politics. In their formative meetings, team members understandably have many "what ifs" about their degree of support in the organization, performance expectations from top management, and their vulnerability if results aren't immediately forthcoming. The supervisor needs to be a channel for whatever assurance and support top management is willing to give to the team. It is crucial that a supervisor's words of encouragement on the part of top management be sincere and trustworthy. A team can be quickly destroyed by reassurances that turn out to be false.

Leadership at a Distance

This final leadership option is practiced most often with executive teams made up of experienced team players. Once given their charter, these self-directed teams are free to achieve their goals (and often define or refine them along the way) in any way that makes sense to the team as a whole. The leader is available to the team for counsel, access to resources, and other forms of support. But, day to day, the leader's contact with the team is minimal. The team reports its results to the organizational leader. If the results meet or exceed expectations, both the organizational leader and team members are rewarded. If not, the team is put on notice by the leader to "hit the numbers" or face dissolution as a group.

This leadership style downplays the potential contributions of the leader to the team in favor of ultimate empowerment of the team itself. For such empowerment to draw the best from team members, it must be *real* in the organization. In the words of one director of a *Fortune* 100 company, "Around here, the authority of our project teams is, at best, ambiguous. We are told 'you can make decisions.' But, in reality, if senior management doesn't like it, it won't fly." In this situation, teams are not really empowered to do their own best thinking and acting, but instead to play an expensive guessing game called "What Does the Boss Want?"

Digital Equipment Corporation stands in the forefront of empowering teams. Managers are trained to respect the expertise of the specialists they supervise, and to let that expertise guide development of products and services. In the words of Geoff Shingles, CEO at DEC, "The role of the manager in the future is going to be to support and coach the experts who are doing the work."[3]

WHAT TEAMS EXPECT OF THEIR LEADERS

No matter whether a leader is designated by top management or elected from the team itself, the members of the team have expectations for the leader's personal qualities and professional skills. In 1994, *Best Practice* magazine summed up seven years of surveys reporting the expectations of team members. In the following percentages, they expect their leaders to be:[4]

- Honest   87%
- Competent   74%
- Forward-looking   67%
- Inspiring   61%
- Intelligent   46%
- Fair-minded   42%
- Broad-minded   38%
- Courageous   35%
- Straightforward   33%
- Imaginative   32%
- Dependable   31%

Note that the highest ratings are given for *telling the truth, knowing the business,* and *anticipating change.* Other qualities that might rank high on a leader's self-expectations (such as "imaginative" or "courageous") end up being of less concern to team members.

Team members also have a right to expect patience and even forgiveness at times on the part of the leader. New ventures and new ways of doing things involve risk for all concerned. If the penalty for mistakes is termination, docked pay, or organizational shame, no team member will give his or her best efforts or ideas to the team process. Deborah Harrington-Mackin, in *Keeping the Team Going,* has collected from managers and supervisors an insightful list of team mistakes that can be pardoned or used without penalty as a learning experience.[5] A team's mistakes can be accepted by management if:

- It doesn't have significant negative impact upon the company.
- It is a first-time mistake, not part of a pattern.
- Team members were working outside the team's responsibilities.
- The team member was following explicit instruction or following the proper procedures.
- The team member was working with shared equipment that is not always available.
- The team learns from the mistake and is able to say how it will be avoided in the future.
- The mistake occurred within the scope of the team's authority in pursuit of the goal.
- The team was really trying to do it right.
- The team's actions were consistent with the policies and rules of the company.
- Incorrect information was given to the team.
- The team was taking initiative and taking risks.
- Procedures weren't clearly defined.
- Different skill and ability levels of team members caused erratic results.
- There were extenuating circumstances.
- The situation was outside the person's control.
- The error was not caused by negligence or lack of action.

- There were time restraints.
- There was poor training.

In effect, the list says to teams, "Mistakes are part of progress." Harold Geneen, former CEO of IT&T, puts the point well: "The best way to inspire people to superior performance is to convince them by everything you do and by your everyday attitude that you wholeheartedly support them."[6]

Feedback for Leadership

Team members may hesitate to give feedback, positive or negative, to the team leader. In some cases, such reticence springs from fear of retribution: the team assumes the leader, who may still be perceived as an authority figure, capable of turning thumbs down on their careers.

But steering a team without feedback is leading without the proper sense of direction. The following "tools" provide a leader with information about how the team perceives and values his or her leadership. In most cases, these tools are used anonymously in an effort to encourage frank, fearless responses.

TOOL 3.1
PERCEIVED INFLUENCE

This tool helps the team and its leader understand the influences of various levels of managers and staff, in rank order, that can affect the team's work.

Instruction:

Circle one number for each of the categories to indicate how much influence each of these categories of employee has on your work as a member of the team.

Category	Very High	High	Moderately High	Some	Little	Very Low
CEO/President	6	5	4	3	2	1
Top managers	6	5	4	3	2	1
Mid-level managers	6	5	4	3	2	1
Team leader	6	5	4	3	2	1
Team members	6	5	4	3	2	1
Subordinates	6	5	4	3	2	1

From these responses, the team leader can assess where and to what degree team members are influenced by various levels of authority within the organization. The team leader should also complete this assessment and compare his or her results with those of the group. The results of this survey can form the basis of a fruitful team discussion.

TOOL 3.2
INTERNAL OR EXTERNAL CONTROL

This tool helps the team determine its attitudes toward the forces that influence decision-making and the extent to which it feels it controls its own destiny.

Instructions:

Select "a" or "b" for each question. If you don't agree completely with either answer provided, choose the one that comes closest to your opinion. After making your selections, transfer your choices to the scoring sheet provided.

1. a. Team members must often deal with issues they do not understand and cannot control.

    b. Team members understand most issues they deal with and have substantial control in their decisions regarding those issues.

2. a. The value of the team's work is usually determined by the hard work and insights of team members themselves.

    b. The value of the team's work usually depends upon how well others in the organization do their work.

3. a. A good team leader is born, not made.

    b. Depending on the situation, any member of a good team can perform well in the role of team leader.

4. a. Teams fail most often due to internal strife and lack of focus.

    b. Teams fail most often because they lack organizational power and support.

5. a. The amount of support given to a team in an organization depends primarily on the intelligence and fairness of top management.

    b. The amount of support given to a team in an organization depends primarily on how well the team makes its case for deserving support.

6. a. The success of a team is often due as much to good fortune or luck as to good work.

    b. The success of a team almost always is due to the quality of its work.

7. a. Teams that make careful plans for their activities usually succeed.

    b. Teams do better to remain flexible, since changes in the marketplace and in organizational priorities usually can't be anticipated.

8. a. Being a valuable team member depends most of all on one's previous level of power in the organization.

    b. Being a valuable team member depends most of all on one's ability to listen well and respond intelligently.

9. a. The work of competent teams is usually rewarded in the organization.

    b. Organizational rewards go most often to teams with the right contacts inside and outside the organization.

10. a. Team skills can be learned by almost all employees.

    b. A significant percentage of employees could never learn to be good team members.

SCORING SHEET

External Influence	Internal Influence
1a _____	1b _____
2b _____	2a _____
3a _____	3b _____
4b _____	4a _____
5a _____	5b _____
6a _____	6b _____
7b _____	7a _____
8a _____	8b _____
9b _____	9a _____
10b _____	10a _____
TOTALS _____	_____

Once scores have been tallied, the team leader can lead a profitable discussion by asking, "Do you consider the team leader an external or internal force, or both?"

TOOL 3.3
ATTITUDES TOWARD LEADERSHIP

This tool will help the team and its leader understand prevailing attitudes about the effectiveness of the leader's role and activities. For each statement, circle one number that corresponds most closely to your opinion.

	Strongly Agree	Agree	Slightly Agree	Slightly Disagree	Disagree	Strongly Disagree
1. The team leader supports my efforts on the team.	1	2	3	4	5	6
2. The team leader is a good listener to problems I face as a team member.	1	2	3	4	5	6
3. The team leader usually goes along with decisions of the team.	1	2	3	4	5	6
4. The team leader makes sure that I am fairly rewarded for my work on the team.	1	2	3	4	5	6
5. The team leader accepts differences of opinion among team members.	1	2	3	4	5	6
6. The team leader helps the team resolve its internal conflicts.	1	2	3	4	5	6
7. The team leader makes good use of time spent in team meetings.	1	2	3	4	5	6
8. The team leader helps team members develop and improve.	1	2	3	4	5	6

	Strongly Agree	Agree	Slightly Agree	Slightly Disagree	Disagree	Strongly Disagree
9. The team leader treats all team members fairly.	1	2	3	4	5	6
10. The team leader leaves many important decisions up to the team.	1	2	3	4	5	6
TOTALS	___	___	___	___	___	___

This instrument should be administered on an anonymous basis. Its results provide a report card of sorts on how the leader is perceived by team members. Once results have been tallied from all members, the scores can form the basis of a frank discussion about areas in which team leadership is effective and ineffective. The discussion should be conducted in such a way that team members do not feel pressured to reveal how they answered particular questions.

Team-Building Tips

1. Acquire the leadership skills needed not only to get the job done right, but to *develop* the people to do it.

2. To determine whether delegated, elected, shared, or distanced leadership is most appropriate for your team, analyze the three P's: your project, your people, and your plans for the future.

3. Remember that teams look to the leader to *tell the truth, know the business,* and *anticipate change* as primary responsibilities.

4. Seek out feedback from the team and those affected by the team not only to measure team performance but also to determine how your leadership role must evolve.

4

Participating
on Teams

*The will to prepare to win is infinitely more
important than the will to win. A team that is
really willing to prepare is the team that has the
best chance to win and wants to win.*[1]

Bobby Knight
Head Basketball Coach
Indiana University

Kodak produces more than seven thousand different black and white film products. The fifteen hundred employees involved in the manufacture and marketing of these products are managed by the "Zebra Team," an elite Kodak unit made up of carefully selected managers, supervisors, and technical experts. Kodak's Executive Committee established this powerful company in 1991 to help restore market share in black and white products that had steadily eroded since the late 1980s. Here's how three team members describe what it's like to participate on the Zebra Team:

"We're crazy. We'll do anything."

"We're so pleased with what we're doing and the results we're getting that we want the rest of the company to learn from us."

"Black and white, black and white. Everybody's a partner."[2]

CONVERTING THE UNBELIEVERS

The enthusiasm and innovative spirit of teams like Kodak's Zebra group stem from rethinking on the part of employees—rethinking how they relate, how they work, and what they can achieve.

Improving an employee's ability to serve as a team member begins by recognizing that many employees resist the idea of joining a team. Jon Katzenbach and Douglas Smith, in *The Wisdom of Teams,* point to three reasons for many employees' reluctance to join teams:

- A lack of conviction that a team approach can work better than other alternatives.
- Personal styles, capabilities, and preferences that make teams risky or uncomfortable.
- Weak organizational support for the conditions in which teams flourish.[3]

Each of these forces can undercut team participation from the beginning, but each presents its own problems and has its own solutions.

Lack of Conviction

Veteran employees inevitably develop firm opinions about and take considerable pride in the "way work gets done around here." It's understandable that, at first blush, they don't rush with excitement to reorganization of work processes using teams. "Teams" for such employees is a code word for what they see as several undesirable developments: changes in their personal work habits and work load, reliance upon others to get work done, and generalized fear of failure. What if the team doesn't meet expectations?

Employees with misgivings must be "sold" on the team concept before they can be expected to participate fully as a team member. This training function may be time-consuming and expensive for a company, but it is exponentially less expensive than forcing unwilling employees to convene as "teams" in name only.

Uncomfortable Personal Styles

Various types of employees resist joining teams due to personal style. Shy, introverted workers may feel that their opinions will never be heard in team discussion. Workers with strong convictions and short fuses may feel that their views will be compromised. Fast-trackers used to "A+" evaluations of their individual work may feel that joining a team can only obscure and even detract from their brilliance.

In all these cases, the key to team success lies in careful selection of team members and initial socialization. Like a child playing with a chemistry set, a company executive can inadvertently put together teams whose members' interaction is guaranteed to be explosive. Or the executive can use skills and ability assessments, role considerations, and careful planning to build a team of complementary qualities. In this environment, each member quickly realizes that his or her strengths are unique on the team and are valued.

Team members should meet one another for the first time in a social atmosphere, even if only in a conference room. Many companies make the mistake of skipping over this get-acquainted step, especially when "most of the team members already know one another." For the sake of even one or two members new to the group, this step provides a chance to get to know others.

Discounted Performance

Imagine an organization in which employees believe that mediocre performance will ensure their continued employment; that superior performance will not help them financially or in terms of career path; and that below-average performance will be tolerated for a long time before relatively mild sanctions are felt. Furthermore, imagine that employees in this organization have made a virtual culture out of mediocrity—that they resist efforts to boost production because improvements in the company's fortunes bring no significant improvement in the fortunes of employees.

Will teams succeed in this organizational environment? No. In the words of Katzenbach and Smith, "All the team-promoting policies in the world will fall short if the teams are not convinced that performance really matters."[4]

THE QUALITIES OF EFFECTIVE TEAM MEMBERS

The most insightful study of effective teams has been that conducted by Rensis Likert of the University of Michigan's Institute for Social Research.[5] Likert studied a wide range of organizations in compiling his list of twenty-four characteristics of effective teams. Suggested guidelines for those seeking to improve their participation in teams are provided in italics.

1. Members are skilled in all the various leadership and membership roles and functions required for interaction between leaders and members and between members and other members. *Team members should therefore seek out cross-training opportunities whenever possible.*

2. The group has been in existence sufficiently long to have developed a well-established, relaxed working relationship among all its members. *Team members should not expect relationships on the team to feel comfortable at the beginning.*

3. The members of the group are attracted to it and are loyal to its members, including the leader. *Team members must be ready to place the welfare of the team ahead of the interests of their former work units and associates in the company.*

4. The members and leaders have a high degree of confidence and trust in each other. *Team members must understand that teamwork is impossible apart from mutual respect among members.*

5. The values and goals of the group are a satisfactory integration and expression of the relevant values and needs of its members. They have helped shape these values and goals and are satisfied with them. *Team members must take responsibility as architects of team culture and conditions.*

6. Insofar as members of the group are performing linking functions, they endeavor to have the values and goals of the groups which they link in harmony, one with the other. *Team members don't enter an ivory tower when they become part of the team. They are influential in the company to the extent that they remain trusted by the groups to which they link.*

7. The more important a value seems to the group, the greater the likelihood that the individual member will accept it. *Team members must expect to be deeply influenced by other team members.*

8. The members of the group are highly motivated to abide by the major values and to achieve the important goals of the group. *Team members discover that their individual performance expectations expand dramatically when they embrace the "one for all and all for one" spirit of the team.*

9. All the interaction, problem-solving, and decision-making activities of the group occur in a supportive atmosphere. Suggestions, comments, ideas, information, and criticisms are all offered with a helpful orientation. *Team members don't try to compete with one another for individual recognition; they contribute for group accomplishment.*

10. In the highly effective group, the leader adheres to those principles of leadership which create a supportive atmosphere in the group and a cooperative rather than a competitive relationship among the members. *Team members learn to look upon their leader in a new way—more as a fellow team member than as a taskmaster or final decision-maker.*

11. The group is eager to help each member develop to his or her full potential. *Team members look upon training as a "must have" for team success, not a reluctant duty.*

12. Each member accepts willingly and without resentment the goals and expectation that the individual and the group establish for themselves. The goals are adapted to the member's capacity to perform. *Team members meet or exceed expectations primarily because they are the architects of those expectations.*

13. The leader and the members believe that each group member can accomplish the "impossible." These expectations stretch each member to the maximum level and accelerate personal growth. *Team members take pride in setting a higher standard and maintaining a faster pace than traditional workers in the organization.*

14. When necessary or advisable, other members of the group will give a member the help needed to accomplish successfully the goals set for that person. Mutual help is a characteristic of highly effective groups. *Team members are ready to assist other team members without judging them.*

15. The supportive atmosphere of the highly effective group stimulates creativity. *Team members recognize that they are empowered to try new things and take risks.*

16. The group knows the value of "constructive" conformity and knows when to use it and for what purposes. *Team members don't sweat the small stuff; conformity to administrative rules and procedures is not viewed as selling out.*

17. There is strong motivation on the part of each member to communicate fully and frankly to the group all the information which is relevant and of value to the group's activity. *Team members don't keep secrets from one another. Knowledge is used for shared power, not personal power.*

18. There is high motivation in the group to use the communication process so that it best serves the interests and goals of the group. *Team members don't brush feelings under the carpet— or burden one another with irrelevant feelings.*

19. Information is welcomed and trusted as being honestly and sincerely given. Members do not look "behind" information and attempt to interpret it in ways opposite to its purported intent. *Team members take each other at face value. They do not impute motives unnecessarily.*

20. In the highly effective group, there are strong motivations to try to influence other members as well as to be receptive to influence by them. *Team members "sell" one another on ideas, information, and perspectives.*

21. By "tossing the ball" back and forth among the members, a group can communicate information to the leader which no single person on a one-to-one basis dare do. *Team members believe their leader is as eager to learn and improve as they are.*

22. The ability of the members of a group to influence each other contributes to the flexibility and adaptability of the group. Ideas, goals, and attitudes do not become frozen if members are able to influence each other continuously. *Team members can't be pigeon-holed according to viewpoints; these change over time.*

23. In the highly effective group, individual members feel secure in making decisions which seem appropriate to them because the goals and philosophy of the operation are clearly understood by each member and provide a solid base for making decisions. This unleashes initiative and pushes decisions down while still maintaining a coordinated and directed effort. *Team members make the decisions that logically should be made at the team level; they do not seek out decision-making power beyond their scope of authority.*

24. The leader of a highly effective group is selected carefully. His or her leadership ability is so evident that he or she would probably emerge as a leader in any unstructured situation. *Team members value their leader and try to support his or her needs.*

GETTING TO BASICS: WHAT TEAM MEMBERS DO AT MEETINGS

Because your on-the-ball team leader has sent you a meeting agenda well in advance of the team meeting, you've had a chance to gather background information and pertinent documents that will be useful at the meeting. You've also had a chance to simply *think*, deeply and creatively, about the issues that will arise at the meeting. Where necessary, you've built bridges by contacting other team members to ask questions, suggest approaches, and indicate concerns.

At the meeting itself, you've learned to speak up early. Research in group dynamics demonstrates that team members who contribute early in a meeting are likely to participate more fully in discussions than those who are silent for the opening minutes.

When you do make your point, cut to the chase right away. Richard Wiegand, professor of management communications at the University of Alabama Graduate School of Business, warns team members against the belief that "they have to fill the audience in on all the background before the major idea . . . can be appreciated. Unfortunately, the group is often half asleep before the big point is revealed."[6]

Even though team discussions are candid and unguarded, you've prescreened your comments to make sure they do not unnecessarily anger or alienate another team member. As Walter Kiechell III recommends in his *Fortune* column, "if you suspect that your assertions on a particular subject may gore another participant's ox, or even nick it, tell him in advance that you are going to raise the issue."[7]

You've also learned (perhaps the hard way) that verbal information is less memorable than visual information. B.Y. Augur, vice president of the Visual Productions Division at 3M, points out that "when relying on verbalization alone to communicate, an estimated 90 percent of a message is misinterpreted or forgotten entirely. We retain only 10 percent of what we hear. But adding appropriate visual aids increases retention to approximately 50 percent."[8]

If the culture of the team doesn't look favorably on slide or computer-generated visual presentations, a simple handout may accomplish your communication purpose without making other team members feel like spectators.

When others speak, you practice active listening techniques by:

- Looking at them attentively.
- Nodding or commenting briefly as a sign of comprehension, not necessarily agreement.
- Taking brief notes as a way of helping your own retention and complimenting the speaker.
- Referring to the previous speaker as a bridge to your own speaking.

What gets said in the meeting and how problems are addressed are the subjects of Chapters 5 and 6.

TOOL 4.1
MEASURING YOUR PARTICIPATION ON THE TEAM[9]

The following tool[9] should be filled out by all team members as soon as possible after a meeting. Compare your responses with those of other team members as the basis of a discussion focusing on improving team communication.

1. Where I sat (sketch):

2. How this seating position influenced my participation:

3. Types of participation (Place numbers in each blank according to the following scale: 1—Agree 2—Not sure 3—Disagree)

    _____ I spoke up to initiate new ideas.

    _____ I spoke up to disagree with other speakers.

    _____ I spoke up to agree with other speakers.

    _____ I spoke up to offer additional information.

    _____ I spoke up with questions.

    _____ I spoke up to clarify points for others.

    _____ I spoke up to summarize points for others.

_____ I spoke up in a humorous way related to the point at hand.

_____ I spoke up in a humorous way unrelated to the point at hand.

_____ I did not speak up.

_____ Other participation: (specify)

4. My attitudes toward participation. (Place numbers 1, 2, or 3, as in the exercise above):

_____ I felt I expressed myself clearly and persuasively.

_____ I felt I expressed myself clearly but not persuasively.

_____ I felt that I did not express myself clearly or persuasively.

_____ I felt that the team usually let me have my say.

_____ I felt that I was usually cut off by other team members before having my say.

_____ I felt that I spoke up too often.

_____ I felt that I wanted to speak up more often, but did not.

_____ I felt that I spoke up too little.

_____ I felt that I communicated an impatient attitude toward the team.

_____ I felt that I communicated a discouraged, cynical attitude toward the team.

_____ I felt that I communicated an upbeat, energetic attitude toward the team.

Team-Building Tips

1. In selecting team participants, be aware of reasons why workers commonly resist membership on a team: lack of conviction, incompatible personal styles, and weak organizational support.

2. Remember that effective teamwork requires mutual respect and trust among participants. Those qualities take time to develop.

3. Don't let an "ivory tower" spirit of superiority or elitism separate the team from the rest of the workforce.

4. As a participant, prepare for team meetings by thoughtfully considering the agenda and planning for your own contributions.

5. Practice active listening to draw the best from other team members and to strengthen the bonds of mutual respect and cooperation.

5

Using Teams
Effectively

*Teams are flexible and responsive to changing
events and demands. As a result, teams can
adjust their approach to new information and
challenges with greater speed, accuracy and
effectiveness than can individuals caught in the
web of larger organizational connections.[1]*

Jon R. Katzenbach
Douglas K. Smith
The Wisdom of Teams

Motorola's growing reputation for quality
and competitiveness is closely linked to
the company's use of teams. Recently, teams

eliminated a bottleneck in testing pagers by using robots, designed and delivered a new computer chip in six months, streamlined the order process for auto electronics, cut production time and the defect rate on a new battery part, cut product development time in half to win an IBM contract, and reduced time required for a training program from five to two years with better results. A *New York Times* article comments, "At Motorola, quality is team sport."[2]

Teams are capable of extraordinary achievements. This chapter highlights some of those achievements.

SUCCESS STORIES

GE Fanuc Automation North America, Inc., is transforming itself into a team-based organization and recently posted its best results ever. The company has been cited by the U.S. Department of Labor as a "clearinghouse organization" for its achievements in team management.

In an industry notorious for poor financial performance, Southwest Airlines has compiled an unrivaled record of 23 consecutive years of profitability. Much of the credit goes to Southwest's teams of ground crews which turn a plane around (unloading, cleaning, reboarding, and departing) in as little as 8.5 minutes. By keeping planes flying rather than sitting around on the ground, teams help keep Southwest's operating costs the lowest in the industry, averaging just 60% of their largest competitors.[3]

Teams at A.O. Smith Corporation's module manufacturing plant have cut manufacturing defects by more than 50% in just two years. Simultaneously, teaming with suppliers has cut the rate of defects on incoming parts by nearly 80% in the same period.[4]

The Maguire Group faced a crisis in 1992 when the company's president was forced to resign for making improper payments to city officials. In response, employee teams developed a corporate-wide ethics policy covering gifts and gratuities, political contributions, entertainment and business expenses, and bribes. The program has been so successful that only one questionable situation has been brought to the Ethics Review Panel since the Code was implemented.[5]

Teams at Alliant Hospital and Healthcare Corporation in Louisville, Kentucky, improved charting of discharges by 50 percent in less than three months while new payroll and tax return processes they developed resulted in savings of $30,000 annually. The Child Life Team was cited by *Child Magazine* as one of several reasons for naming the Alliant Hospital as one of the 10 best Children's Hospitals in America, and the Post Anesthesia Care Unit (Recovery) team eliminated $8,300 annually of on-call pay by rewriting the process for weekend call-ins.[6]

At Lesher Communications, a newspaper printing company in northern California, teams have reduced the plant's crucial measure of paper cost per ton from the baseline of $222.78 to $197.47, even though total work and tonnage increased over the same period. Given current figures, plant managers expect the paper cost-per-ton figure to drop to $150, thanks to the success of the plant's self-managing teams.[7]

Cincinnati-based uniform maker, Cintas, makes about 60,000 garments per day, 11 million annually. For 25 years, Cintas has enjoyed an annual compounded growth rate exceeding 20 percent and net income has increased more than 25 percent per year for the past 25 years. Company officials attribute their success to high-tech equipment, team-based modular manufacturing, and a corporate culture that emphasizes long-term success.[8]

These extraordinary accomplishments and others from reports in professional journals and newspapers are testaments to the effectiveness of teams when they are implemented properly. Effective implementation doesn't happen by accident. Decision-making and problem-solving strategies based on optimum organizational features and project characteristics required for successful use of teams are available to organizations.

PROBLEM-SOLVING AND DECISION-MAKING STRATEGIES

It's easy to overlook the continuous nature of decision making and problem solving in organizations because they are such commonplace activities. Procedures for both are built into the very structure of organizations. One study reported that an average employee in a typical organization makes as many as 1,400 decisions every day! As long as the situations are familiar, decisions are made and problems are solved in routine ways that attract little attention. Only when situations are out of the ordinary— exceptions to common practice—are we likely to think about the ways they are managed. Otherwise, we let normal organizational processes run their course without paying attention.

Today, the changing environment is forcing many organizations to reconsider their basic decision-making and problem-solving strategies. It is common to distinguish three distinct strategies: individual decisions, use of advisory groups or committees, and team-based approaches. You have probably seen each work in your own organization and it's unlikely any real organization doesn't use a mix of the three. Each has its advantages and disadvantages, and each has a role in a comprehensive approach to making decisions and solving problems.

Individual Strategies

Without a doubt, individual decision-making and problem-solving is the most prominent pattern in organizations. The majority of routine, and many non-routine, decisions are made by individuals.

The defining characteristic of individual strategies is that a single person makes the decision and is responsible for its outcome. In the purest form the individual makes the decisions without consulting others or seeing additional information. More commonly, the person may rely on subordinates to gather information and may seek advice from peers, colleagues, consultants, or other experts. But, even in this modified form, the individual decision-maker determines who will be involved, how their input will be used, and what the final decision will be. And, he or she alone is responsible for the outcome.

Many businesses have evolved on a military command-and-control model emphasizing individual strategies. This approach has served them well and is still appropriate in many situations. Specifically, individual strategies are appropriate when the situation is:

- structured

- limited in scope

- subject to time pressure

- within the decision-maker's competence or expertise.

A problem is said to be "structured" when there is a defined procedure for dealing with it. Balancing a checkbook is a good example: the procedure is clearly defined and almost everyone is familiar with it. Similar examples include processing routine customer orders, and generating income statements and other financial documents.

A situation is said to be "limited in scope" when it falls entirely within one individual's area of responsibility and authority. In traditional structured organizations, individuals at lower levels have narrowly limited and strictly defined areas of responsibility, while those higher up the pyramid have broader, less clearly defined responsibilities. However, the principle remains the same regardless of the individual's level in the organization: as long as the situation is wholly within his or her area of responsibility or authority, an individual strategy may be appropriate.

Whenever a decision must be made quickly, individual action is often preferred because a single individual—at least an informed individual who is close to the situation—may solve a problem before a team can even be assembled. Of course, individuals are more likely to make errors than well-prepared teams, but (within limits) there is no substitute for individual action when prompt response is required.

Competence or expertise is an important consideration. As long as the responsible individual is sufficiently knowledgeable or can readily consult with others who have appropriate technical expertise, there is little reason to form an advisory committee or team.

Individual decision-making and problem-solving strategies are the most economical and efficient, and their use is appropriate whenever a situation can be resolved through a structured process, is limited in scope, imposes time pressure, and falls within the individual's area of competence. These characteristics aptly describe many situations, but an increasing number fall outside these bounds and call for other strategies.

Advisory Groups and Committees

Individual decision makers routinely consult with others, but the formation of an advisory group or committee is a significant departure from informal conversations with friends, colleagues, and advisors. While advisory groups and committees do not have the authority to make a decision, their recommendations carry more weight than advice solicited through informal means, and executives may be called upon to justify decisions that depart significantly from a committee's recommendations. Moreover, advisory groups and committees often have formal procedures, a broad range of constituents, and periodic meetings that shape the decision process.

Advisory groups and committees are used to their best advantage when:

- Many points of view are relevant.
- Broad areas of knowledge or expertise are required.
- Time is available to permit study and discussion.
- There is good reason to control the resulting decision.

The ability to represent many points of view is a principal reason for using advisory groups and committees. Members are deliberately chosen to represent different constituencies, and recent thinking on corporate governance has emphasized the importance of serving multiple stakeholders. For example, a corporate policy advisory group might include representatives of labor, management, local residents, stockholders, and relevant regulatory agencies.

Advisory committees can be especially effective for problems requiring broad areas of knowledge or expertise. Marketing high-tech products is a good example, and an advisory committee may well include market research specialists, electronics engineers, production engineers, and venture capital consultants.

Quick response is not a hallmark of group processes. New groups need time to develop roles and procedures before dealing with a significant issue. Even established groups may need several hours to get up to speed on a problem and significantly more time—perhaps weeks or months—for its members to conduct relevant research or poll their constituencies.

Advisory groups are preferred when there is some reason to control or limit the decision-making powers of individual members. This is often the case when members of the committee do not fully share the objectives of the parent organization. For example, labor union representatives may oppose significant changes in work rules, or community activists may oppose plant relocation. Hearing their views is important, but it would be a mistake to let them alone make the final decision.

Team-Based Solutions

Team-based solutions can be viewed as the third link in the chain. They fill a niche bounded by individual strategies and advisory groups. Specifically, team-based solutions are most appropriate when the problem is unstructured, calls for many points of view, requires broad areas of expertise, and group members share the interests of the parent organization.

Decisions marked by these characteristics are not uncommon and there is a growing tendency to employ team-based strategies. However, teams are not infallible and the performance of decision teams shows that they are not always the ideal approach to problem solving.

MAKING TEAMS WORK

While both formal research and everyday experience consistently document the value of teams, team-building is not without its problems. Four factors may impinge on the effectiveness of a team's functions.

Social Tension

The term *primary tension* refers to the natural uncertainty most people feel in a strange situation. Group activities remain a novelty for many people, and most feel some tension when they participate in team activities for the first time. This tension, like "stage fright," is a very normal response to performing in an unusual environment and usually lessens with familiarity.

While everyone experiences primary tension, some groups encounter a more serious problem commonly called "secondary tension." Secondary tension is the result of struggles between group members and may manifest itself in several damaging behaviors:

- unexpected outbursts and shouting matches at team meetings
- limited participation or complete withdrawal by selected team members
- deliberate attempts to sabotage team activities

Primary tension is caused by uncertainty about expectations in a new environment and is best managed through activities that familiarize members with the team environment: introducing members and giving them time to become comfortable with one another; explaining the nature of the project and the procedures that will be employed; and, simulated problem-solving activities.

Secondary tension generally has its roots in problems outside the team and is characteristically the result of long-standing personality conflicts, struggles for power and dominance, and efforts to enhance an individual member's status. Normal team building activities will help minimize some of these difficulties, but it is generally necessary to confront them directly with the aid of a skilled facilitator. In extreme cases, it may even be necessary to reconfigure the team by replacing one or more members and bringing in new participants who have similar competencies but less "baggage." Both primary and secondary tension must be dealt with if a team is going to be effective.

Cohesiveness

Cohesiveness refers to members' feelings about the team. It reflects the degree to which members like being on the team, and it shows up in the ability of team members to get along with one another, and feelings of loyalty, pride, and commitment to the team.

In general, cohesiveness is an asset, and highly cohesive teams are often more productive than other groups. Research indicates that higher levels of cohesiveness are associated with more communication between members, friendly cooperative climates, greater ability to influence behavior, and higher levels of member satisfaction.

These are all positive features, but there appear to be some limits. Research on the relationship between cohesiveness and productivity indicates that it is possible to "have too much of a good thing." Beyond a threshold which has yet to be clearly defined, highly cohesive teams turn into social clubs that emphasize membership and participation at the expense of performance. In other words, higher levels of cohesiveness are associated with higher levels of productivity up to a point beyond which productivity declines while cohesiveness continues to grow.

Some highly cohesive groups fail to maintain a high level of performance either because (1) the team has accomplished its original objectives and has not filled the void with new goals or objectives; and/or (2) team members lack conflict management skills to tackle tough issues and have fallen back on essentially social activities to avoid painful confrontations. Either situation calls for renewed team building: establishing new goals and objectives in the first case and developing conflict management skills in the second. One additional option is to disband.

Groupthink

Occasionally, members of highly cohesive teams become so focused on a single course of action that they refuse to consider either alternatives or potential difficulties. Labeled "groupthink" by Irving Janis, this phenomenon has been well-established and well-documented. Janis demonstrated that groupthink was responsible for inferior decision-making processes that culminated in a number of historic fiascoes. The danger of groupthink is ever-present; teams should be ever vigilant in watching for the symptoms.

1. The illusion of invulnerability—a belief shared by team members that the team cannot make an error.

2. An unquestionable belief that the team is above ethical or moral restraints and that their decisions are inherently moral.

3. Collective rationalizations that lead team members to discount information that is inconsistent with their assumptions or decisions.

4. Stereotyped views of competitors that suggest they are incapable of responding effectively to team initiatives or proposals.

5. "Self-censorship" which effectively prevents members who disagree with team decisions from speaking up.

6. An illusion of unanimity which implies that all members of the team agree with decisions even though some may have spoken in opposition.

7. Pressure to conform applied to members who argue against team stereotypes, illusions, or commitments.

8. The emergence of "mind guards"—members who protect the group from discordant information.

These features inhibit a team's decision-making ability by limiting the amount of information and number of alternatives considered, and by creating barriers to critical thinking.

All teams are at risk of groupthink, and effective teams guard against it by ensuring that all members are free to speak their minds, actively soliciting outside opinions and expertise, postponing decisions until alternatives have been carefully considered, and appointing devil's advocates to argue against premature consensus.

Group Polarization

Research has indicated that groups may make more extreme decisions than individuals confronted with the same problem. Some researchers have called this the "risky shift" phenomenon, and the following example is characteristic. A manufacturer is preparing to release a new product and market research has suggested four possible production levels, each with different assumptions about potential demand, ranging from a low of 1,500 units to a high of 6,000 units per month. Groups are significantly more likely to pick one of the extreme values than individual decision-makers who typically choose intermediate values.

While the extreme values may actually be correct, guarding against the inherent tendency of groups to pick bolder solutions is a never-ending task. Carefully reviewing information and arguments for and against proposals, soliciting advice from outside experts, developing procedures well, and learning from experience are the best protection.

PROJECT CHARACTERISTICS AND ORGANIZATIONAL ENVIRONMENT

Skilled teams have effective ways of coping with each of the potential team-building problems. However, developing countermeasures takes some time and the decision to use a team should be carefully weighted. The following pages present a model designed to help you make the decision. As you will see, teams are best used when both project characteristics and organizational features are appropriate. Teams may be used in other situations, but the results are often disappointing.

Project Characteristics

Teams are appropriate for projects that have one or more of the following characteristics:

- They are perceived as worthwhile to team members.
- They are not highly structured *and* routine projects. A project that has both of these characteristics is not the best use of a team approach. Some projects, such as new product development, have highly structured processes, but the problems they tackle are anything but routine.
- Projects that call for knowledge or expertise beyond the scope of any one individual can benefit from a team-based approach.
- The project appeals to members' individual interests and match the goals of the organization.

Organizational Environment

Some organizational environments, like some projects, undermine effective teamwork. Three elements in particular can be used to gauge whether a team has a reasonable chance of success or not:

1. Support and encouragement of key management and staff.
2. Freedom from undue outside influence or interference.
3. Access to adequate resources.

Teams need the active support and encouragement of key managers and staff. When they set expectations and confer authority clearly, provide adequate resources and support, and clear roadblocks, they build the foundation for successful team performance and success. Team members must be encouraged to explore and consider solutions beyond the prevailing views of the organization.

But managers often have difficulty letting go and, as a consequence, essentially sabotage team efforts. Teams are more likely to succeed when they are free from undue outside influence. One disgruntled former team member described the experience:

> Management talked a lot about teams and teamwork. They even hired a consultant to teach us how to work together. We were all pretty excited at first, but it didn't last long. Ten minutes into the first meeting, we could see what was really going on. Management had already figured out what they wanted and all the team stuff was just window dressing. They wouldn't let go, and we gave them the answer they wanted. We all knew it wouldn't work, but they just wouldn't listen to us. Nobody was surprised when it blew up in their faces and I say it serves them right! I'll never sit through another farce like that and I'm already looking for another job.

Organizations often limit or even prevent a team's success by not providing proper resources. Such resources include:

- Sufficient staff with appropriate skills and abilities.
- Planned time for meetings and work sessions.
- Ready access to information and outside expertise.
- Appropriate tools and equipment.
- Adequate budgets.

THE IMPACT OF PROJECT CHARACTERISTICS AND ORGANIZATIONAL ENVIRONMENT

Wonderful things happen when teams are suitably used for projects in supportive climates. Figure 5.1 summarizes the probable outcome of team projects under different situations.

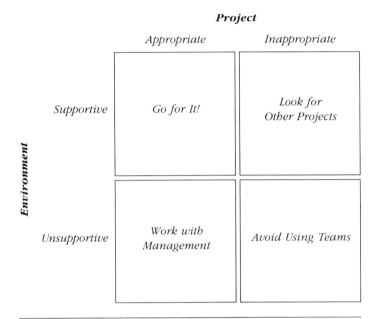

FIGURE 5.1
DECISION MATRIX FOR USING TEAMS

CHAPTER

6

Problem-Solving with Teams

Whenever possible, we move toward consensus because people feel more involved and empowered, and they take greater ownership of the decision.[1]

> John Hofmeister
> Vice President, Human Resources
> Allied Signal Aerospace

The NUMMI auto plant in Fremont, California, is the decade-old joint venture between General Motors and Toyota. The average work team at NUMMI consists of 6 to 8 members. A team leader, who is paid slightly more than the rest of the team, functions as the "utility" player for the team by filling in for absent workers and helping those who fall behind in their work. Cords hang alongside the high-tech production line throughout the NUMMI plant. If any worker spots defects or other problems, he or she is empowered to shut down the entire production line by pulling a cord. Teams offer suggestions on how work can be distributed most advantageously, and bonuses are given to teams and individual workers whose suggestions improve efficiency. To date, the NUMMI operation consistently achieves the highest productivity and quality levels of any U.S. auto plant.

———————

Much of the success of teams like those at NUMMI can be attributed to a well-crafted problem-solving process. Team members must understand this process. Groups, with members without such focus and orientation, typically fall into one of two dysfunctional syndromes.

Some groups fall into a circular pattern and discuss whatever is on the participants' minds at the moment. They make progress slowly, if at all, because decisions are never final, so issues are never settled. With everything potentially on the table at once, these groups reopen questions that should have (and might have) been answered earlier. When new topics or issues are raised, they are simply added to the mix and compete for attention with everything the group has considered previously.

Other groups follow a more linear pattern marked by strong emotions and wasted energy, dubbed forming, storming, norming, and performing. Members get to know one another and agree about virtually everything during the first phase. The second phase is marked by strife and group members disagree about everything; even trivial topics provoke strong disagreements which limit opportunities for effective discussion. Members establish norms or rules of conduct during the third phase, and serious problem solving takes place only during the fourth phase. Groups that follow a linear pattern are slightly more productive than those that follow a circular pattern.

These two patterns are so prevalent that some management experts have concluded that they occur naturally. While we agree that they are the most common, we believe that the best teams, in contrast, employ a carefully crafted process distinguished by five elements:

- Building and renewing the foundation for effective teamwork.
- Employing a structured problem-solving process.
- Employing specific problem-solving tools.
- Measuring their results.
- Designating a process champion.

TEAM-BUILDING: ESTABLISHING AND RENEWING THE FOUNDATION

Identification of a shared sense of mission and great expectations, the use of commonly accepted procedures, and providing and accepting continuous feedback: these attributes are the foundation of effective team performance.

Out of Many Members, One Team

All teams begin as groups of individuals with their own concerns and perceptions of the team and the project. Psychologists refer to these factors as "entry variables," and all groups have them when they are assembled for the first time. Significantly, many groups never become more than a collection of individuals. Molding a loosely gathered bunch into a cohesive team is the first step in the team-building process. Here are two approaches that have worked well for us.

Expanded Personal Introductions

Introducing members of a team to one another or giving members an opportunity to introduce themselves is a commonplace way to begin a new team. We like to expand on the process by giving group members something specific to talk about. We often facilitate this introduction process by administering and discussing a personality inventory such as the Team Member Selector found in Appendix 2 or, if time allows, the more extensive Myers-Briggs Personality Type Indicator (MBTI). These instruments focus directly on the members themselves. From the beginning, we want the team to recognize, accept, and value individual differences.[2]

We begin the meeting with a brief explanation of the team process and ask members to introduce themselves. Then we distribute copies of the MBTI and explain that there are no right or wrong answers. And, we assure everyone that the results will be confidential; they are free to share as much or as little as they like. Then, we ask everyone to complete the MBTI, working by themselves.

It generally takes around 45 minutes for everyone in a typical group to complete the MBTI and calculate the results. Once everyone has finished, we explain the four preferences revealed by the MBTI and the 16 personality types depicted. When everyone is satisfied that they understand their own results, we begin an open discussion by writing our own personality types on a flip chart and reading the descriptions aloud. As we read the descriptions, we emphasize the elements that are particularly important in understanding how we respond to situations.

After reviewing the descriptions of our own types, we ask each member to follow suit, disclosing their own types, reading the descriptions aloud, and emphasizing important elements or questioning features that may not be true of their approaches. As each member presents their type, we note it on the flip chart so that we have a list of all the types represented on the team once we finish the round robin.

When everyone is finished, we review the team profile posted on the flip chart. We want everyone to be thinking about their own profile, the profiles of their colleagues, and the composite team profile. We then encourage participants to comment on two features of the composite profile:

- What are the unique strengths of this team? That is, what preferences are well represented on the team?
- What are the potential weaknesses of this team? That is, what preferences are not well represented on the team?

Properly done, the whole process requires about 2 1/2 hours, but participants always believe the time has been well spent. They particularly like the objective discussion of individual differences, the expanded awareness of their own preferences, and the enhanced ability to understand their colleagues' approaches.

The MBTI is an extraordinarily powerful tool for building a cohesive team and we use it often.

Simulated Problem-Solving and Decision-Making Tasks

A second approach to building a team involves the use of simulated decision-making and problem-solving activities. Pencil and paper "survival exercises" are popular, and the fact that there are objectively correct answers makes it possible for team members to identify procedural errors which they will try to avoid when handling real problems.

"Lost on the Moon," first developed by NASA, is the grandfather of written survival exercises and has spawned a large family of similar commercial instruments. Here's how the exercise works. Team members are presented with a particular problem like this:

> Your space ship has crash landed on the moon. Your only chance of survival is to travel some distance to a place where your mother ship will be able to locate you. You have salvaged 15 items from your space craft but you will not be able to carry all of them with you. In the column marked "your choice" rank order the fifteen items from 1 (most useful) to 15 (least useful).
>
> After everyone in your group has finished, work with your colleagues to reach consensus on rank ordering the fifteen items. Use the column "group's choice" to record the group's decision. The following is a sample.

	Your Choice	Group's Choice	NASA's Ranking	Your Score	Group's Score
Box of matches					
Food concentrate					
Parachute silk					
Solar-powered portable heating unit					
Two 45-caliber pistols					
One case of dehydrated milk					
Two 100-pound tanks of oxygen					
Stellar map of the moon's constellation					

After all of the participants work out their own solutions, they work with their teammates to develop a group solution. Then the facilitator presents the correct answers and participants calculate four scores:

- Best individual score in the group.
- Worst individual score in the group.
- Average score of individual in the group.
- Group score.

We suggest that teams grade their performance as follows:

Grade	Group score is:
• A:	better than the best individual score
• B:	better than the average individual score
• C:	roughly equal to the average individual score
• D:	worse than the average individual score
• F:	worse than the worst individual score

Groups generally have a great deal of fun completing the exercise, and B is the most common grade. Real learning takes place when members begin thinking about how process affected their decision making. When we lead the exercise, we help groups create two lists:

- Behaviors or approaches that helped them make appropriate decisions, and
- Behaviors or approaches that reduced their effectiveness.

Survival exercises and other simulated decisions help team members understand one another and focus attention on the processes they use. Lost on the Moon generally takes around 2 hours while commercial versions require from 2 to 8 hours. Representative sample problem-identification instruments are presented in Appendix 1.

Recharging the Team

Over time, teams get tired and the factors that contribute to effective teamwork erode. Effective teams recognize the danger and periodically set aside time to recharge. Virtually any activity that allows team members to spend time together without concentrating on work-related problems will do. Social gatherings, sporting events, and social service projects are examples.

Structured Problem-Solving Process

Consistent use of a structured problem-solving and decision-making process is the second hallmark of the best teams. Whenever we introduce the concept of structure in classes or seminars, someone will usually ask the question: "Isn't structure inconsistent with creativity?"

No matter how the questions are phrased, underlying them is a fundamental misunderstanding about the role of creativity in team processes. Creativity and structure work hand-in-hand to promote outstanding results. The key is understanding when structure facilitates or stifles creativity and effectiveness.

Creativity is appropriate when teams are looking for innovative ways to define a problem, generating potential solutions and searching for novel ways to implement a solution. During these phases, creativity is essential and appropriate. At other times, teams need to be anything but creative. Developing detailed problem descriptions, systematically evaluating proposals, and carefully planning implementation processes call for a structured approach.

Effective teams employ six steps designed to promote creativity, when appropriate, or structure, when needed.

Step 1: Defining the Problem

Defining the problem is the first step in every problem-solving process. It is a critical step because the definition establishes the boundaries of the problem, the kinds of data needed, and the range of solutions. Here's a case that emphasizes the importance of an adequate problem definition.

> A team was asked to simplify a particular step in a complex manufacturing process. After several meetings and a good deal of hard work, they produced an impressive list of possible solutions with price tags for equipment and training up to $120,000. However, they had failed to ask whether or not the step was even needed, and later realized that they should have focused on the entire process rather than on a single step. When they expanded their horizons, they realized that the process itself was archaic and the step with which they began could be eliminated completely, saving countless headaches and considerable money.

This is an extreme example, but it has been our experience that many teams spend too little time defining problems. In contrast, the best teams work diligently to make sure they have an adequate definition before proceeding to the next step.

Defining the problem should culminate in a simple, one-page statement describing the specific problem the team intends to solve. The step isn't finished until all members of the team agree that it is a clear statement of the problem. In addition, it is often appropriate to get reactions from higher management and other affected groups. Their input may result in expanding or contracting the definition to include all relevant concerns.

Step 2: Describing the Problem

Once a problem has been defined, the next step should focus on describing it in detail. Every problem has both a quantitative and qualitative dimension, but it is at this stage that "putting a number on it" can be extremely helpful. Appendix 1 at the end of the book contains samples of a few methods for gathering information about a problem. Different techniques are better-suited to different types of problems, but at this stage detailed information is very important to determine various stages and degrees of a problem. Many statistical measures can be used to develop information and understanding about a problem. This information should enable the team to answer the following kinds of questions:

- When was the problem first observed?
- How often does the problem occur?
- Who is affected?
- How severely are they affected?

Although teams often feel pressure to get on with the next step, effective teams avoid moving to the next step until they have a substantive body of information to identify the root causes of the problem and to lay the groundwork for developing the best solutions.

Step 3: Developing Possible Solutions

Developing possible solutions is the third step, and there is a predictable sequence of activities. Most groups begin by generating a list of solutions that have been discussed previously and are familiar to most members. These "stock" solutions generally lead to disagreement, with members quickly taking sides. Left unchecked, discussion will quickly turn to the merits of each solution. Strong teams know that this is a critical moment in the problem-solving process. Team members must suspend judgment until a longer list of potential solutions has been generated.

Once they are over this hurdle, other possible solutions can be identified. This third step should produce a long list of potential solutions. Effective teams regularly push themselves through all three stages because they understand that truly creative and innovative solutions are most likely to emerge after commonplace suggestions have been voiced and everyone begins looking for something more.

Step 4: Selecting the Most Promising Solution

Selecting from among the potential solutions calls for thoughtful discussion and judgment. High-performing teams work systematically to find the most promising solution to satisfy the problem. These teams avoid three potential traps at this stage.

Taking the easy route is the first trap. After very little discussion, one solution may seem ideal and team members will tend to jump at it without considering potential obstacles or other equally worthy alternatives. Teams can skirt this trap by carefully reviewing all of the alternatives before making a selection. They take even greater care when one solution appears to be the overwhelming favorite, and they search for its flaws as well as its selling points. In extreme cases, they may even appoint a "devil's advocate" to make sure both pluses and minuses are fully voiced.

Votes, the second trap, are so widely used in our society that they seem to be the democratic way to resolve all issues. While they are commonplace, votes are seductive traps and generally lead to inferior results. Team members on the losing side are less likely to commit themselves to effective implementation of the chosen solution.

Enforced consensus and coalition formation are the third trap. When feelings run high, teams may break into warring sides. Those who disagree are pressured to conform, which further compromises the quality of the decisions and undermines the team's cohesiveness.

Step 5: Planning and Implementing the Solution

Many great ideas are never fully realized because of inadequate implementation. Once a decision has been made, care must be taken not to pass on responsibility for its implementation to someone else.

Effective teams know that implementation is as critical as finding an appropriate solution. They are far less ready to relinquish responsibility and often insist on having a role in implementing their proposals. Once a solution has been selected, they proceed to outline the key implementation steps, establish deadlines, assign responsibility for completion of each step, and monitor progress.

Step 6: Evaluating Performance

Strong teams treat the conclusion of each project as an opportunity to improve their own team processes. While ordinary teams take a break between projects, exceptional teams use this time to review their procedures, garner feedback, and search for ways to improve their individual and collective performance.

SPECIFIC PROBLEM-SOLVING TOOLS

Effective teamwork is rigorous and demanding, but teams don't need to invent the specific tools they use. Teams can employ a well-honed set of tools that have proven their value in countless situations. Some of the most common are displayed in Table 6.1 and a more complete set as well as directions for their use are presented in Appendix 1.

TABLE 6.1

Problem-Solving Step	Appropriate Tools
1. Defining the problem	Brainstorming Problem Census Man from Mars
2. Describing the problem	Man from Mars Tally Sheet Check Sheet Run Chart Histogram (Bar Chart) Scatter Chart Pie Chart Customer Survey Employee Survey Financial Reports and Projections Marketing Reports Customer Chain Analysis Cause-Effect (Fishbone) Diagram
3. Generating possible solutions	Brainstorming Topic Census Nominal Group Technique
4. Selecting the best solution	"T" Graph Screening
5. Planning implementation	Action Plan Project Management Grid Gantt Chart
6. Evaluating the results	Brainstorming Topic Census Nominal Group Technique Screening

DOCUMENTATION

Time is among the most valuable team resources. A carefully thought out agenda helps them manage time during meetings, and action plans orchestrate their work between meetings.

Agendas

Effective teams would not even consider conducting a meeting without an agenda. They know that agendas are invaluable guides to using time wisely and insuring that essential tasks are completed.

While run-of-the-mill teams use haphazard lists to organize their meetings, the best teams use a specific form that indicates what will be discussed and what kind of action is required, who is responsible for making the initial presentation, and how much time has been allocated for each item. The following is a typical agenda.

A G E N D A
MANAGEMENT TEAM MEETING
February 7, 19__

2:00–2:15	Personnel has asked us to select two senior staff members to describe our marketing program to the trainees in the Management Training Program. We need to decide whether or not we will participate and select speakers if we decide to participate.
2:15–2:45	We have been asked to review the proposed R&D budget and recommend possible changes.
2:45–3:15	Mark Hamilton will announce the results of our promotional effort and distribute copies of the annual report.
3:15–3:40	The Corporate Services Division has proposed a 21-hour course in Effective Managerial Communication. We need to decide if we are going to participate and what fraction of the expenses we are willing to pay.
3:40–4:00	Accounting has developed new procedures that require more elaborate reports. I've asked Marsha Harrington to describe the DP services available to us and summarize their uses.

Agendas are generally prepared by the team leader, but all members should be prepared to contribute. The following items are based on the experiences of members who regularly use extended agendas to guide their work. Some teams use it as a checklist.

1. Include only items whose resolution is consistent with the functions of the group: receiving information, developing recommendations, and making decisions.

2. Limit meetings to no more than two hours; longer meetings are less productive than several short ones because attention wanders and participants tire rapidly.

3. Schedule items requiring creativity for the first twenty or thirty minutes; discuss routine items during the concluding portions of the meeting.

4. If meetings often drag on, schedule them for the hour or two immediately before lunch or at the end of the work day.

5. While you are preparing the agenda, solicit topics from the participants. Including topics of concern to them avoids the disruptive effects of "hidden agenda."

6. Do not use the heading "other business." The time required by unanticipated items is uncontrollable and participants may be unprepared to discuss topics not on the agenda.

7. Distribute the agenda two or three days prior to the meeting. This is enough time for participants to prepare, but not so much time that the agenda is mislaid or forgotten.

8. When background reports are scheduled, include the name of the person making them so that other members can volunteer information prior to the meeting.

9. Phrase agenda items in a neutral manner so that your preferences do not influence the group.

10. Include references to source material or reports that the participants may consult prior to the meeting and bring with them.

Action Plans

Team meetings are most productive when individual members are fully prepared to participate and have done needed research or fulfilled other obligations to the team. As a result, effective teams seldom close a meeting without preparing an action plan. An action plan is nothing more than an agreed-upon list of things that must be done before the next meeting and the person(s) responsible for completing them. Specific tasks depend on the nature of the project, but typical items on an action plan include finding, summarizing, and distributing relevant information; inviting selected outsiders such as senior executives, technical staff members, consultants, or other experts, vendors, or customers; testing or otherwise evaluating products and services the group is considering; and composing, editing, and distributing interim reports.

Action plans need not be formal, and many teams use a simplified table like this one:

Team Name _____

Date _____

Person Responsible	Task	Deadline
_____	_____	_____
_____	_____	_____
_____	_____	_____
_____	_____	_____

Other features may be added, but this contains everything required.

PROCESS CHAMPION

Effective teams make sparing use of outside facilitators. While they recognize that someone skilled in group processes can make a substantial contribution to their performance, they prefer to develop the necessary skills within the team. To accomplish this objective, they often appoint a process champion, a member of the group who is willing to set aside his or her feelings about the topic and concentrate on the procedures used by the team.

When feelings run high, the process champion is typically the team leader or another respected member of the team who has already developed sophisticated facilitation skills. When things are likely to be less intense, the process champion may be a less-accomplished member of the team who is appointed for the express purpose of developing his or her skills.

In either case, the process champion plays the same role an outside facilitator does. Principal tasks include the following:

- Orchestrate the entire meeting, clearly stating its purpose and distributing an agenda prior to the meeting.

- Summarize appropriate procedures and make sure the team sticks with them when emotions might otherwise divert activity.

- Ensure that the meeting room is adequately prepared with sufficient seating, flip charts and easels, paper, markers, masking tape, and other items.

- Discourage disruptive behaviors and emphasize double-loop procedures when interpersonal problems surface.

- Observe and interpret group dynamics and provide members with specific, nonthreatening feedback regarding their conduct and contributions.

Team-Building Tips

1. Initiate all team projects with team-building activities to prepare the group for the task ahead.

2. Periodically provide time and initiate activities needed to reestablish the elements of effective teamwork.

3. Approach all problems with a structured methodology that includes defining the problem, describing it in detail, developing possible solutions, selecting the most promising solution, planning and implementing the solution, monitoring progress, and evaluating team performance.

4. Use proven problem-solving tools to support team activities at every step of the problem-solving process, documenting the problem and plans for its solution.

7

Trouble-Shooting Team Obstacles

We aren't where we want to be, we aren't where we ought to be, but thank goodness we aren't where we used to be.[1]

Lou Holtz
Head Football Coach
University of Notre Dame

"We followed a high-paid consultant's advice and organized our work processes around teams. Perhaps we expected too much too soon. The fact is that work flow and decision-making slowed dramatically, as teams got used to working with one another and had meetings, meetings, meetings to deal with even small decisions. After about six weeks the company grapevine was carrying the message loud and clear: 'This team thing just doesn't work.' We convened our executive committee to make a decision whether to struggle on with the team organization or to go back to our traditional work roles and reporting order.

"Before we made that decision, however, we took time to investigate what had gone wrong with our teams. We discovered three problems: we hadn't trained employees to work as team members, we hadn't revised the pay and bonus structure in the company to reward teamwork, and we hadn't realized that new ways of working would yield new kinds of results, not the same deliverables we were used to. Instead of scrapping the teams, therefore, we invested money and time in a two-month intensive training program for all employees, top to bottom. We haven't ironed out all the wrinkles, but we're definitely seeing progress in the form of morale, innovation, and flexibility to meet changing market conditions."[2]

In the many books and articles on teams, this frank narration of "problems in paradise" is rare indeed. Hundreds of companies are happy to publish stories about their successful teams for every one company willing to tell about team failures. There's no way of measuring precisely, but it would be a safe estimate that at least half of all team experiments in American corporations are unsuccessful. In many cases, these companies quietly go back to their old ways of doing business.

Perhaps the best advice when establishing teams in an organization for the first time is that of Al Davis, general managing partner of the Raiders football team: "A great leader doesn't treat problems as special. He or she treats them as normal."[3] Problems in the initial stages of team formation are growing pains. It's not necessary to give up on the promise of teams at the first sign of trouble.

When problems do surface among team members, between the team and its leader, or between the team and the organization, skilled trouble-shooting can help the team overcome its obstacles.

PROBLEM 1: DISRUPTIVE INDIVIDUALS ON THE TEAM

Every team needs a non-conformist—one who is willing to express unpopular opinions and to ask uncomfortable questions. These members help the team avoid groupthink and contribute positively to the team's work.

Other individuals, however, behave in ways that are disruptive to the team and destructive to its mission. The team leader or, preferably, the team itself must deal with these individuals fairly, but firmly. Consider five problematic team members, along with suggestions on how to deal with them.

The Team Leak

This team member violates the trust of other team members by a constant stream of memos to management ("I want to bring to your attention . . ."), phone calls ("I just thought you needed to know that . . ."), and letters to the company newsletter. The Leak takes items from confidential discussions—often speculative ideas or tentative planning—and publishes them to the rest of the company as if they were already fact.

Once these acts have been committed, the interpersonal damage within the team itself is difficult to repair. Team members may never trust the Leak again, and may go so far as to hold secret meetings at which the Leak isn't present. When the Leak is present at meetings, discussion may be guarded and the work pace may slow. The team and its leader must decide if the potential contributions of this person to team goals sufficiently outweighs his or her removal from the team. If the Leak stays, retraining may be necessary to help this individual and the team understand how to handle team-related information appropriately.

The Sphinx

This person sits silently through most team meetings. His or her attitude is generally doubtful, if not downright cynical, about the team's efforts and processes. Even when other team members attempt to draw the Sphinx into discussion, he or she gives short and noncommittal responses, making clear that participation on the team is a matter of "have to," not "want to" for the Sphinx. Only when things go wrong does the Sphinx speak up, or signal nonverbally: "I told you so."

Like the Leak, the Sphinx damages the work of the team by dragging down morale. A potentially positive approach to dealing with a Sphinx is to assign this person an important, but manageable, aspect of a team project that requires the Sphinx to report regularly to the team. This combination of greater participation, responsibility, and visibility encourages some Sphinxes. Some find that working with the team instead of against it is more fulfilling.

The Word Hog

Often, Word Hogs haven't worked closely with a team before. In their enthusiasm to contribute, they over-do and, consciously or unconsciously, deprive other team members of their chance to participate. Just as often, Word Hogs come from management ranks and think of themselves as having the last word, as well as the first, on virtually any topic. It isn't that their input lacks value. What they say may be factually correct. But they subvert the possible synergy that comes from a diversity of opinions.

The team and its leader can often tame the Word Hog by taking him or her aside to point out this behavior. If personalities make this impossible, many team leaders have resorted to keeping a one-minute egg-timer handy. Whenever a team member's contribution starts to verge into a lecture, the egg-timer comes out to remind one and all (usually in a humorous way) to get to the point and then give others a chance.

The Contrarian

As mentioned earlier, there is a valuable place for the "loyal opposition" in any team process. But the Contrarian raises objection to an obsession. This individual gains attention by sparring intellectually and emotionally with other team members on each and every point. Most of these objections are quibbles that add nothing to the team's discourse. They are objections simply for the sake of objection.

One approach to this kind of individual is for the team leader or some members to tell the Contrarian in constructive and frank terms how he or she can contribute more productively to the work of the team. The goal of such a confrontation, of course, is to guide the Contrarian to more positive ways of relating, not to discourage his or her input altogether. Another, more positive approach to handling this individual is to give him or her a leadership role in some aspect of the team's work. When the Contrarian has a positive assignment to complete and present, he or she is much less likely to spend meetings taking potshots at others.

The Buzzer

The Buzzer talks about shopping, the weather, traffic conditions, company politics, and what's for lunch—virtually any topic not associated with the team's goals. A team leader can try the polite approach once or twice with the Buzzer. If that suggestion doesn't work, the team itself can agree to stop discussion entirely when a buzz of extraneous conversation occurs in the background. When silence falls in the meeting, the Buzzer has no camouflage of sound to hide behind. He or she will usually be sufficiently uncomfortable to pipe down and get back on track with the team discussion.

Problem 2: The Runaway Team

Many teams make the mistake of exceeding the scope of their authority. Other teams have limits on their activities and authority. The team's responsibilities and authority need to be defined clearly—and early in the process.

The key in dealing with a runaway team lies in directing their activities without squelching their morale and energy. This can be done by avoiding direct criticism of their work. Instead, rechannel their energies toward the problem or task at hand.

Problem 3: The Do-Nothing Team

At the other end of the spectrum from the Runaway Team is the Do-Nothing Team—the team that meets and meets, drafts memos and outlines future reports, but never seems to accomplish meaningful work or produce results. These groups have lost their focus by too great a concern for team processes, such as consensus-building, participation by all members, and organizational learning. Although these matters are important, at some point, deliverables must be due and deadlines must be met.

The most common solution for the Do-Nothing team is the least adequate: a top level manager lays down the law and tells the team what it must achieve, and when. This approach does lead to action on the part of the team, but it also undercuts the value of team concept itself. Better that the team itself should be guided (by an external manager or its own leader) to evaluate its progress, make hard decisions about its use of company time, and come to an agreed-upon action plan for more timely accomplishment.

Problem 4: The Divided-Loyalties Team

Especially when cross-functional teams have been assembled from highly competitive, cohesive divisions within the company, it is likely that members will consider themselves temporary emissaries to the team from their "home base" rather than as loyal team members.

These concerns are best addressed by a communication system promoted by top management, which keeps all divisions informed about the work of cross-functional teams. Company newsletters, executive briefings, on-line company magazines, and up-date memos can all play a part in letting company employees learn about team activities and successes.

PROBLEM 5: THE TEAM IN TURMOIL

Even after managers have selected presumably complementary members for a team, the interpersonal chemistry between members can be wrong—and explosively so. The Team in Turmoil is one that cannot meet for more than 15 minutes without shouting matches or seething silences.

Understanding the causes of turmoil on a team is comparable to untangling a wad of yarn. It does little good to pursue all leads at once—that merely tightens the knot. Instead, choose one or two members of the team for a meeting with you. Assure them of confidentiality. Try to ascertain, in a nonthreatening way, the real nature of the conflict besetting the team. Have two members divided the team into enemy camps? If so, forging a truce between those individuals may resolve the turmoil on the team.

If the conflict centers on more than two people, look for issues that keep tempers flaring. Perhaps aspects of the team's goals statement are perpetual irritants to many team members. In that case, consider altering the goals statement if advisable, or realigning the team with new members more suited to the goals statement.

Finally, the root of turmoil on the team may lie in the members' conflict with the team leader. Your conferences with a few team members will quickly bring this information out in the open. If the leader clearly is at fault, additional training or help in distributing leadership functions within the team may be good alternatives to outright replacement.

PUTTING SOLUTIONS INTO ACTION

Andrew Leigh and Michael Maynard, British experts on team processes, recommend that trouble-shooters consider nine ways to bring teams and team members back into productive work:[4]

- Praise: For everyone, especially those who respond to immediate feedback. ("That was excellent because . . ."; "Well done!")

- Leading Questions: For people who respond to a signal or need to overcome their reticence. ("Don't you think that . . .")

- Explanations: For people who are motivated by understanding the reasons for doing something. ("The reason is that . . .")

- Requests: For people who like to be asked. ("I have a difficulty. Next time could you . . .")

- Advice: For people who prefer guidance or are influenced by the logic of the situation. ("Next time you might try . . .")

- Promises: For people who find the task unattractive or need extra motivation. ("If you succeed, we will . . .")

- Orders: For people needing exact instruction and where compliance is essential. ("Do it now. It must be done this way . . .")

- Criticism: For people who respond to negative feedback. ("What you did wrong was . . .")

- Threats: For people who do not respond to more positive methods, and where compliance is essential. ("If you don't do it this way . . .")

Obviously these approaches to influence and motivation must be suited carefully to the individual and situation at hand. Trouble-shooters should also remember the ripple effect of any of these methods: word will travel quickly through the team and beyond about what you said and how you said it. A threat issued to one team member may, through the grapevine, grow to larger proportions as a threat against the entire team. It is often better to talk to the entire team at once so that each member knows exactly what you said and meant.

TWELVE SYMPTOMS OF TROUBLED TEAMS

Most problems don't always present themselves unambiguously. The first signs of trouble on the team may be subtle. The following "devil's dozen" can help sharpen your eyes and ears to the early symptoms of a team in distress:

1. Watch for team members who seek individual recognition rather than recognition for the entire team. These members are the people who usually feel "We had to do all the work ourselves."

2. Listen for complaints from individual members who feel they had to go along with the majority on the team in spite of their own opinions. Team members voting against their best judgment and conscience are time bombs that, over time, will explode in words and actions.

3. Observe the "bench" players who sulk on the sidelines because they don't like the way things are going on the team. These withdrawn and often apathetic team members are trying to tell you something about the team.

4. Pay attention to team members who always seem to be pouring oil on choppy waters. These members are averse to conflict, even when it is productive, and will do all they can to make sure the team is a "happy family," no matter what the implications for getting good work done.

5. Spot the "blamers" on the team, particularly those who chastise the leader for all the team's problems. These are typically the people who will not accept responsibility for challenges but are more than willing to accept praise for accomplishments.

6. Watch for isolated entrepreneurs on the team—those who are bent on setting their own goals and choosing their own methods, no matter what the feelings of the rest of the team.

Although innovation and originality are certainly to be encouraged on the team, these qualities can't be used as an excuse for loose-cannon behavior on the part of individual members.

7. Listen for inappropriate "talking out of school" by team members. These individuals may seek out managers and other co-workers as a audience for their tales of woe about team mistakes and internal difficulties. Whistle-blowing about significant problems is vital to a company's well-being, but indiscriminate criticism of fellow team members destroys trust and respect within the company.

8. Weigh the message being sent by individual team members who want to bring their clones onto the team as new members. This effort to stack the deck with one personality or role type usually indicates the beginning of a power play on the team by individuals who, through insecurity or inability, feel they must accomplish by numbers what they cannot accomplish by cooperative effort.

9. Watch for signs of impatience on the part of some team members who can't or won't spend time discussing how the team functions. These members are usually the ones who are first to break the unwritten rules on the team regarding full participation in discussion, respect for opposed points of view, and the value of consensus in decision-making.

10. Take careful note of team members or entire teams who turn in half-baked work or consistently miss deadlines, often with excuses about inadequate time, resources, or assistance. If these excuses are legitimate, the team surely should have notified you earlier in their work. After-the-fact excuses are symptomatic of teams unable to complete their assignments no matter what levels of support they are given.

11. Track absenteeism. Team members may be speaking volumes about their attitude toward team goals and processes by arriving late, leaving early, or missing meetings altogether. These members always seem to have the best of reasons, of course. But there's no excuse for a continuing pattern of absences.

12. Look for signs of premature celebration on the part of some team members. These individuals seem to feel their work

is done once the team has settled on its approach to a given problem.

TROUBLE-SHOOTING THE TROUBLE-SHOOTERS

Those who investigate team problems are often the same people responsible for the team in the company's reporting order. In looking for culprits, these investigators often must echo Pogo's famous line, "We have met the enemy, and they are us." *Today's Team Facilitator* magazine recently published ten ways in which those responsible for teams are also the primary causes of the team's problems. Here's what may be going wrong at the top, with negative effects cascading through teams at all levels in the company:

To ensure team failure as a manager:

- Don't listen to any new idea or recommendation from a team. It's probably not a good idea since it's new and different.

- Don't give teams any additional resources to help solve their problems in their area. Teams are supposed to save money and make do with less. Besides, they probably will just waste more time and money.

- Treat all problems as signs of failure and treat all failures as reasons to disband the team and downgrade team members. Teams are supposed to make things better, not cause you more problems.

- Create a system that requires lots of reviews and signatures to get approval for all changes, purchases, and new procedures. You can't be too careful these days.

- Get the security department involved to make it difficult for teams to get information about the business. Don't let those team members near any computers. You don't want them finding out how the business is run.

- Assign a manager to keep an eye on the teams in your area. Tell each member that he or she is there to help facilitate (teams like that word). But what you really want these managers to do is control the direction of the teams and report back to you on any deviations from your plan.

- When you recognize or change policies and procedures, don't involve team members in the decision or give them any advance warning. This will just slow things down and make it difficult to implement the changes.

- Cut out all training. Problem-solving is just common sense anyway, and besides, all that training really accomplishes is to make a few consultants really rich.

- Express your criticism freely and withhold praise and recognition. People need to know where they have screwed up so they can change. If you dole out praise, people will expect a raise or reward.

FINAL THOUGHTS ON TROUBLE-SHOOTING

Organizations small and large have made the mistake of converting to team-based work without planning for ways to deal with inevitable team difficulties. A company can't simply hope that things will go well with teams, or rely on the success of teams in other firms. The trouble-shooting function that ensures quick, expert attention to team problems must be given high priority and strong support in the company. Teams are worth the effort.

Team-Building Tips

1. Treat team problems as normal, not special. Problems are an inevitable part of desirable processes of change and adaptation.

2. Be prepared for five common team problems: the disruptive individual, the runaway team, the do-nothing team, the divided-loyalties team, and the team in turmoil.

3. Watch for the twelve symptoms of troubled teams. These signal a wise leader to take early action.

4. Troubleshoot the troubleshooters, making sure that those responsible for teams are not also those causing the team's major problems.

8

Technology for Teamwork

Effective organizations are open to change and committed to innovation. Instead of trying to minimize or resist change, these organizations encourage and nurture change and learn how to manage it so they can take advantage of the opportunities it presents.[1]

> Don Mankin, Susan G. Cohen,
> and Tora K. Bikson
> *Teams and Technology*

The 777 airplane is Boeing's latest entry into the highly competitive global aircraft marketplace. This plane is the largest twin-engine aircraft in commercial service and carries a price tag of over $100 million. Each 777 is nearly 210 feet long and has a wingspan just short of 200 feet. It consists of 3 million parts. With a gross weight on takeoff of 250 tons, the 777 can carry as many as 440 passengers, 4,800 miles without refueling.

To create this marvel, Boeing divided its employees into 238 design-build teams, each responsible for a section of the airframe or a major aircraft system. Teams were staffed by experts from all areas of airplane development, including Engineering, Production Procurement, and Customer Support. Teams included representatives from customers and suppliers. Subcontractors were located in 12 states and 10 foreign countries. In a fitting tribute to outstanding teamwork, the first prototype 777 was just .023 inches away from perfect alignment along its entire length, even though it was assembled in Washington State from sections made in Kansas and Japan.

Boeing's accomplishment is extraordinary. Fortunately, the technology that made such teamwork possible is increasingly available to companies large and small and is applicable to all kinds of situations, whether they are technology-driven (like Boeing) or not.

The Internet

As we have mentioned in previous chapters, one of the key problems facing every team is the problem of undue outside influence. "Good" influence—expertise provided by a non-team member—is or always should be welcome. Undue influence is a different matter—and it's often based on access to information or expertise. The Internet can increase a team's independence, and it can help avoid undue influence. The Net gives team members direct and near-instant access to sources of expertise and information from all over the world.

The Internet was created in the 1960s by the Advanced Research Project Agency. It was originally intended to provide a secure communication network for scientists and technicians, and it was anything but "user friendly." Users had to master arcane commands and the most common applications were electronic mail, electronic bulletin boards and file transfers.

Over time, new uses have merged and new tools have been created to attract larger audiences. Each new application has been added to earlier generations of tools and it is best to think of the Internet as a "network of networks" with multiple tools and connections to huge corporations, commercial services (e.g., CompuServe and America OnLine), independent service providers (ISPs), and individual computer users.

Today, users still encounter earlier applications, including ftp (file transfer protocol), Telenet (virtual terminal protocol), WAIS (wide area information server), as well as Archie and Gopher, search tools designed to locate information on earlier generations of the Internet. While each of these continues to serve specific functions, development of the World Wide Web supporting graphical browsers such as Mosaic and Netscape Navigator has made the Internet an information resource far richer than imagined by earlier generations of users. Recent studies indicate that the number of users is expanding by 15 percent per month and World Wide Web traffic is growing exponentially.

The dramatic growth of the Internet is paralleled by a literal explosion in the quantity of information available. At least 20,000 businesses have established Web sites to distribute information about their products or services as well as the status of ongoing research projects. In addition, major university libraries and the Library of Congress have made their catalogs available on line, while academic and commercial research centers regularly post their findings along with detailed analyses and "white papers." Finally, community, state, and federal government agencies freely distribute information such as census data and current corporate 10K and 10Q statements. All of this information—and more—is there for you and your team's use. And, you can read it on line, print it for your files, or download it for subsequent inclusion with appropriate credit in your own work.

TELECONFERENCING

Teleconferencing is a general term and refers to several technologies that permit members to participate in team meetings without being physically present. There are now three common forms with a fourth on the horizon.

The growth of teleconferencing has been accelerated by two factors. First, there is a growing tendency to create teams that include members who cannot regularly attend meetings. For example, it is often desirable to include members who have special expertise but are based at other facilities. Moreover, many organizations have found it beneficial to include customer and supplier representatives on selected teams even though travel costs would be excessive. In these circumstances teleconferencing is a practical way to conduct team meetings even though members may be scattered around the globe.

The need to respond to uncontrollable circumstances and costs is the second reason for the increasing use of teleconferencing. Any number of events can prevent members from traveling to attend team meetings and force companies to use alternate strategies, including telecommuting and teleconferencing.

Audioconferencing

Audioconferencing is the easiest and least expensive form of teleconferencing. While voices are the primary medium of exchange, they can be complemented with fax transmissions so participants have copies of critical documents and other materials.

Audioconferences require few special resources and they can often be set up with a little advance preparation. However, other forms of teleconferencing offer much more and audioconferences are best thought of as emergency measures when other forms are unavailable.

Textconferencing

Computer-based textconferencing is the second common form of teleconferencing. Participants use personal computers connected to a common network and appropriate software, and each may contribute ideas or information, review other participants' contributions, and edit a common document.

Various hardware and software configurations are available, but most divide each user's computer screen into a number of separate windows. Text-based conferencing can be quite effective once members are familiar with the medium and comfortable working with other participants who are unseen and perhaps unknown. However, there is a general movement toward approaches that add video images of other participants and related materials.

Videoconferencing

Videoconferencing is today's state of the art. Contemporary systems range from low-end units, which simply add a video camera to a personal computer and display images of other participants in windows on the monitor, to high-end systems with elaborate studios and large screens.

In spite of the variations, it is useful to distinguish between stop-action and full-motion video. Stop-action systems (or "slow scan" or "capture video") employ relatively slow data transmission rates that may be carried over traditional phone lines. These systems are best used to display documents, models, or other stationary objects.

Full motion video systems employ faster transmission schemes that require more capable and, hence, more expensive hardware and network connections. They present video images at higher speeds and are comparable to what you would see on commercial television. Displayed on life-sized monitors, these images can create the feeling that other participants are physically present and generally contribute to more lively discussions.

While corporations have spent hundreds of thousands of dollars creating videoconferencing suites, there are economical alternatives. Personal computers can be outfitted for low-end videoconferencing for less than $2,000, and commercial videoconferencing suites in a growing number of cities can be rented on an hourly basis.

Cyberconferencing

Each of the teleconferencing tools described above is readily available and may be put to work for you right now. The most recent innovation, full scale "cyberconferencing," is still experimental, but holds promise as a fourth form of teleconferencing. Cyberconferencing uses the latest generation of virtual reality tools to create images of the participants and a virtual conference room in which the meeting takes place.

A recent trial brought together participants in Japan and the United States. Each participant was outfitted with virtual reality goggles connected to powerful computers and a common network. When the system was switched on, participants found themselves seated around a conference table with "avatars," computer representations of the other participants. One window in the conference room looked out on Mount Fuji while the other presented a vista of Mount Rainier, and the participants were able to engage in normal conversation with one another while playing a game that involved herding around a group of cyber-animals on the surface of the cyber-conference table.

While the trial was designed to test the limits of the technology, participants were able to do everything required to conduct a face-to-face meeting. With continued development, cyberconferencing is likely to emerge as a fully capable replacement for conventional meetings.

RESOURCES ON CONVENTIONAL NETWORKS

Local area networks (LANs) have been a feature of modern corporations for some decades and they have established their value as means of sending email, posting notices, transferring files, and sharing access to data bases. Properly employed, they facilitate dramatic improvements in efficiency, but their accomplishments appear minor compared to the contributions of "groupware."

Groupware burst on the corporate scene in 1990, most notably in the form of Lotus Notes® and early studies indicated that it could reduce the amount of time required to complete some projects by as much as 90 percent. Formally defined, groupware is an integrated set of network tools that facilitate group communication, planning, decision making, and other cooperative efforts. Typical installations include the following:

- Networked word processing tools that support shared files, cooperative text revision, and control of different versions of each document.

- Networked spreadsheets designed to enhance collaboration by permitting shared access to files, simultaneous editing, and instant updates with corrections made by one user are immediately available to other users.

- Cooperative schedule programs that find available meeting times and automatically notify users when meetings are added to their calendars.

- Networked project management tools that can be updated by all team participants and automatically note delays and other variances from plan.

- Email with mailing lists so that messages can be directed to all members of a team as well as broadcast features that facilitate rapid distribution of news updates and other information.

- Computer conferencing facilities which support multipoint participation in text conferences.

- Group support features such as electronic whiteboards, online outliners, brainstorming and decision-making routines, and

- Concurrent access to databases with user-friendly front ends including graphical user interfaces.

In addition, the best-of-breed groupware programs provide a platform for the development of company- or team-specific applications.

The real significance of groupware is that it has redefined the kinds of interaction possible over networks. Whereas earlier programs supported one-to-one or one-to-many distribution of static messages, groupware facilitates simultaneous dynamic many-to-many exchanges.

This expansion of communication opportunities is exactly what teams need, and it can be applied to virtually any situation a team faces. The following examples give a good idea of the types of problems to which groupware can be applied.

- Problem: A consulting team has less than a week to submit a proposal to a prospective client, but the consultants are currently on assignment in several states and two foreign countries.

- Groupware Solution: Conferencing facilities allow team members to develop a common perspective while the networked word processor allows each to compose specific sections of the proposal and cooperatively edit successive drafts. In addition, linked data bases help them identify the most capable consultants for the assignment and review prior projects to create baseline schedule and pricing data.

- Problem: A team composed of representatives from several different functional areas needs to develop a new quality management program. Although all of the members are based at the same location, they have different work schedules and representatives from Sales and Marketing are frequently out of the office.

- Groupware Solution: Integrated scheduling software makes it possible for them to find time for face-to-face meetings as well as computer conferences. Integrated data bases provide information regarding current quality standards and customer reactions while decision support tools help them develop a unique program and identify available resources. A networked spreadsheet is used to develop the program budget while a networked word processor helps them document the program. At every step, their work is coordinated through an online project management program and email allows them to share important developments and maintain contact with senior executives overseeing the project.

• Problem: A product development team includes representatives of several departments as well as suppliers and distributors located overseas.

• Groupware Solution: A cooperative scheduling program helps them find time for meetings and online conferences while a networked project management program tracks their progress. Coordinated data bases provide data concerning the potential market, customers expectations, and competitive products as well as materials and manufacturing costs. Email is used to report internal and external developments while a networked spreadsheet is used to develop budget and return figures and a networked word processor helps to document their work and prepare marketing materials.

• Problem: A senior executive team is reviewing annual budgets as well as capital allocation proposals that impact on several remote facilities.

• Groupware Solution: A networked spreadsheet allows each to share the results of what-if analysis with other team members while email and conferencing facilities make it possible for them to coordinate their analyses as well as secure input from executives at the remote facilities. As their review progresses a networked word processor

allows them to simultaneously edit their recommendations to prepare convincing rationales for their
decisions.

INTRANETS: THE NEXT-GENERATION CORPORATE NETWORK

While conventional networks support a variety of tools that assist
teamwork, they may become obsolete as "intranets" emerge as
the dominant form of corporate network. As the name suggests,
intranets are internal corporate networks employing Internet
protocols. Some observers have suggested that Lotus Notes® is
dead and Marty Zisman, one of Lotus's two chief executives,
is reported to have said that the rapid deployment of intranets
is "the one thing that keeps [him] up at night." He seems to have
good reason for concern:

- 89 percent of organizations responding to the 1996
  Network World 500 study have or will have an
  intranet strategy for their company in the next 12
  months and 73 percent already have Web servers
  for intranet applications,

- a recent survey found that 22 percent of *Fortune*
  1,000 companies now use intranets compared to
  virtually none in 1994,

- another survey found that intranet sales accounted
  for 43 percent of the $1.1 billion 1995 market for
  Web servers and predicted that 1997 sales will top
  $4 billion,

- Netscape says that 70 percent of its sales are for
  products used on intranets and more than half of its
  third quarter 1995 revenues were from sales to
  companies establishing internal webs, and

- The Business School of Harvard University recently
  replaced its six conventional networks with a single
  intranet.

Describing technical differences between intranets and conventional networks is beyond the scope of this book, but you should be aware that intranets have significant advantages. Intranets are easier to deploy and maintain because they readily connect different types of computers. Mainframes, minicomputers, work stations, PCs and Macintoshes can operate on the same intranet and the widely anticipated network PC will be optimized for intranet applications. Moreover, intranets are significantly less expensive than traditional network applications. Programs cost far less than groupware applications and training expenses are minimized by the intuitive, graphical browsers available. In addition, existing computers may be connected and the proposed $500 network PC will be far less expensive than conventional computers.

Given these advantages, it is easy to see why a growing number of companies are using intranets. Here is how some of them are using intranets to support collaborative work.

Morgan Stanley

The investment bank Morgan Stanley has linked its 37 offices around the world and about half of its 9600 employees are connected. The intranet is used primarily for information dissemination and electronic messaging, and the firm believes the system solves a problem they have "wrestled with for many years." Producing and distributing a daily report on Morgan Stanley's positions in a variety of bonds and the latest interest rates offered in Tokyo, London, and New York is a primary information dissemination application. Prior to deployment of the intranet, employees in New York worked until midnight cutting and pasting a 100-page daily update which was then faxed to traders and brokers worldwide. With the intranet, most of the data are culled from databases and assembled on a web page without any human intervention, and the document is updated continually so traders get the latest information.

Morgan Stanley is also using the intranet for electronic messaging, creating a global intercom telling traders and sales people what securities to buy or sell. The voice message system used prior to deployment of the intranet broadcast information on desktop speakers, but employees were always in danger of missing important news when they were away from their desks. With the intranet, each announcement is digitized and stored on a web server so that traders can play and replay messages merely by logging onto the web.

Chief Information Officer Kevin Parker says that the system has been so successful that he plans to add the investment banking and mergers and acquisitions departments to the web, once security software is in place.

AT&T

AT&T is using an intranet to connect its employees to applications such as a system that integrates disparate billing systems from various AT&T business units, an interface to library services, internal research, external news feeds, a system for ordering office supplies, and an employee-contacts database.

The company believes use of the intranet has dramatically changed the information distribution model within the company. Prior to deployment of the intranet, information was "pushed" to employees regardless of their particular needs, but now information is "pulled" by employees who go to the information they need. For example, employees can locate colleagues using POST, an internal database of phone numbers that lets users work their way interactively up and down organizational levels by just pointing and clicking.

Similarly, the Information Services Network organization has developed a Web interface to a library network that provides access to traditional library services such as book loans, photocopies, and reference services, as well as expanded services such as internal document handling and database access. In addition, AT&T Bell Labs distributes nearly 5000 technical papers every year and all are available online. The Web page also lets employees access news feeds for a number of information sources including DowVision and the Associated Press.

AT&T is simultaneously moving to digital cash which allows employees to draw credits from their existing billing system and use a universal transaction system to buy services from other units. AT&T believes that this will enable the company to remain decentralized while eliminating the overhead associated with decentralized billing systems. For example, employees now order office supplies right from their desktops with our global procurement system employing a Web interface that sports a drag-and-drop, Java-based interface to an office supply catalog.

Eli Lilly

Headquartered in Indianapolis, Indiana, Eli Lilly develops, manufactures, and sells pharmaceutical products in 120 countries worldwide, and is using an intranet to distribute information to its 30,700 employees. The goal of the virtual information network is to make information easily available to everyone who needs it, and employees can access information such as internal job postings, bulletin boards, phone directories, press releases, corporate policies, computing policies, the daily stock price, and a news feed on the pharmaceutical industry. Specific applications include distributing product and sales information to up to 300 sales people worldwide, and a prototype forms-based system for its sales representatives to use when calling on hospitals, doctors, or other health care providers.

McDonnell Douglas

Based in Long Beach, California, the 11,000-person Douglas Aircraft Company, a division of McDonnell Douglas Corporation, builds airplanes for over 200 airlines around the world. In addition to delivering airplanes, it delivers a staggering volume of aircraft service bulletins that average 25 pages. The service bulletins provide crucial information on modifying and servicing the company's planes, and the Douglas delivers four or five each day to customers around the world. This amounts to over 4 million pages of documentation every year, and McDonnell Douglas has begun to distribute the bulletins electronically. According to the company, the intranet based distribution system is:

- Less expensive because electronic distribution costs less than half the cost of managing paper.

- Faster because customers receive service bulletins immediately instead of waiting two to three weeks for materials to reach international customers.

- More flexible since customers can integrate the files directly into their own documents, and more durable since digitized documents can be saved indefinitely whereas paper copies have a finite life span.

The security of proprietary information is a major concern, but use of Netscape's Commerce Server allows McDonnell Douglas to encrypt data using RSA encryption. To view or download service bulletins, customers simply call up McDonnell Douglas's home page and choose a button labeled "Access Service Bulletins." They then are required to enter their unique password.

Team-Building Tips

1. All teams should have access to contemporary communications resources including the Internet, teleconferencing, and network support with advanced groupware or intranet programs.

2. Audioconferencing is inexpensive and readily available, but is most useful as an emergency measure when more advanced forms are unavailable.

3. Computer-based text conferencing can be effective, but there is a growing tendency to use systems with video displays.

4. Videoconferencing is today's state of the art and low-end systems can be added to networked PCs for around $2,000 each while leased facilities are economical alternatives to corporate video suites.

5. Groupware is a valuable addition to any team's arsenal. It can be used to establish meeting times, track ongoing projects, develop recommendations and budgets, and support team-specific applications.

9

Supporting the Team

The question isn't "How do we get our teams right so the organization can be more effective?" The question is "How do we get the organizational system right?" When you get your system right, you find many situations where teams don't work and others where they do.[1]

Jack Gordon, Editor
Training Magazine

Once upon a time (in 1892, in fact) there was a small company founded on the idea that research into applications of electricity could prove profitable. Thomas Edison was attracted to the company as a director in 1894. The little firm began to grow until, by the late 1980s, it was the sixth largest corporation in the U.S. and the tenth largest corporation worldwide. Like a giant spreading oak, the company had extended its limits into hundreds of markets.

Unfortunately, the company had grown large but not strong. Employees complained that they were caught up in "the system," making independent initiative difficult if not impossible. The giant oak was showing signs of decay.

The company was General Electric, and CEO Jack Welch was not about to let it fall into the malaise that had gripped so many U.S. corporate icons, including Sears, K-mart, Apple, and others. Welch announced his approach to revitalizing the company in a letter to GE stockholders in 1990:

> Change is in the air. GE people today understand the pace of change, the need for speed, the absolute necessity of moving more quickly in everything we do. . . . From that pursuit of speed . . . came our vision for the 1990s: a boundaryless company. Boundaryless is an uncommon word . . . one that describes a whole set of behaviors we believe are necessary to achieve speed. In a boundaryless company, suppliers are not "outsiders." . . . Every effort of every man and woman in the company is focused on satisfying customers' needs. Internal functions begin to blur. Customer service? It's not somebody's job. It's everybody's job.[2]

Welch was describing teamwork. Under his leadership approximately 40 percent of General Electric's workforce of 120,000 now work in teams of some kind, double the number involved in teams in 1989. The team concept isn't a fad or experiment at GE. Teams have a direct impact upon the bottom line. According to Robert Erskine, manager of production resources at GE: "We're trying to radically reduce the work cycle needed to produce a product. . . . When you combine automation with new systems and work teams, you get a 40 to 50 percent improvement in productivity."[3]

Teams work so well at GE because the company devoted the time and money to preparing work attitudes and behaviors for this radical change in work arrangements. As in the GE experience, teams do not spring from a corporate vacuum. Preparations of many kinds must be in place if teams are to fulfill their promise in an organization. This chapter describes the preconditions necessary for effective teams—in effect, the network of support that nurtures and sustains teams.

TRAINING, TRAINING, TRAINING

For much of the modern business era, the training function has been the poor cousin within most companies. Training, in a word, was often considered marginal to the "real work" of the company.

By 1990, and especially after the publication of Peter Senge's bestselling work on organizational learning, *The Fifth Discipline,* companies took a new view of their training departments. Instructors now faced the daunting challenge of bringing employees up to speed not only in technical skills, but also in a broad range of interpersonal skills, abilities, and attitudes.

The toughest nut to crack for these training departments remains the most important: how to convert a traditional employee to a flexible, motivated team player. That training goal for the rest of the decade and into the new millennium will certainly occupy the majority of training time in companies converting to team-based work.

What is the curriculum for training team players? By whatever titles, training programs across industries emphasize four topics:

Self-Direction

Traditional employees, since their first jobs, have been trained to take direction from the boss, not to generate their own marching orders. Even when they have had some experience in developing operating procedures on committees and task forces, these employees still know little about establishing goals and mission statements. Training departments therefore have the double challenge of undoing old assumptions about the nature of work and instilling, through conceptual and experiential lessons, the skills necessary for self-direction as participating team members.

Valuing Complementary Talents

Workers traditionally have been segregated according to abilities and roles—all technicians in one group, for example. Most have grown used to working with a homogenous rather than heterogeneous peer group. Especially if these employees have not been exposed to personality type inventories (see Chapter 2), they may fail to appreciate the value of diverse personality types and talent sets on a team. Trainers have the often difficult task of convincing these traditional workers to accept diversity as a value, not a hindrance, to teamwork.

Mastering New Administrative Responsibilities

Traditional workers usually have little experience in keeping up with the administrative aspects of work. Matters such as budgets, hiring, and performance evaluation were the domain of the manager. Trainers now face the challenge of teaching these workers not only how to stay within a budget, but how to create one, negotiate for resources in the organization, hire necessary personnel, and monitor performance through fair evaluation procedures. Self-directed teams do assume these responsibilities because, lacking authority in these areas, the team would be paralyzed in its ability to establish and fulfill its goals. But getting employees ready for these added tasks isn't easy, especially when employees have grown used to thinking of administrative details as "someone else's" responsibility.

Developing Cross-Functional Skills

Boundaries of member responsibilities are blurred in effective teamwork. The technical specialists on the team can't opt out of giving management ideas any more than the managers on the team can take a hands-off attitude toward technical issues. In Matthew Arnold's phrase, the "best thoughts of the best minds" are supposed to be active on the effective team, with no artificial classifications or role definitions to limit team discussions and action. Trainers must change workers used to saying "that's not my job" to team members willing to say "it's our job."

REALIGNING RESOURCES

Executives serious about supporting company teams should perform a simple, but telling activity: list the major kinds of resources available to support work in the company. Then ask the question, "Which of these can easily be accessed by our teams?"

Let's say, for example, that a list of company resources includes money, product information, market information, support staff, technical assistance, training support, and access to external experts. A well-supported team should be able to draw upon these resources, within limits, to achieve its goals. Given this resource list, the team should not run into brick walls and endless red tape in funding its budget, having direct access to company data bases, bringing aboard secretaries and other staff as needed, arranging for technical expertise, writing its own ticket for training, and hiring consultants.

Unfortunately, companies often fail to realign resources for easy access by teams. No matter how compelling their ideas, teams are thrown back into the "beggars before the king" paradigm in asking for necessary support. Empowering members of teams means, at heart, giving them the keys to the company larder—and holding them accountable for effective and judicious use of what they take.

PERFORMANCE EVALUATIONS AND FEEDBACK

But how will you be evaluated? There's the rub. Many companies set teams to work before answering this crucial question. Will team members evaluate one another? Will the success or failure of the team's efforts determine the performance evaluations of all its members? Or will the company vice president or other executive attempt to evaluate the work of each team member independently?

This thorny question underlies the willingness of workers to join company teams as well as their motivation in performing team tasks. Consider four approaches to developing fair performance evaluation procedures in advance of the creation of company teams:

1. Use the Management by Objectives method of evaluation to negotiate agreed-upon goals with the team as a whole. Team members understand that they swim or sink together. Becoming a member of the team means in this case linking your financial fortunes and career path to the performance of other team members.

2. Follow the principles of self-direction in asking the team to come up with its own legally defensible ways of evaluating the performance of its members. Some teams may assign this responsibility to the team leader. Other teams may use consensus decision-making or silent vote to give "superior," "good," "adequate," and "inadequate" ratings to members. (In all such evaluation systems, of course, detailed written descriptions of behaviors should be given to support the evaluation and provide suggestions for improvement.)

3. Team members can be asked to write up a self-evaluation of their work, perhaps following categories provided on a standard

evaluation form. In this option, members must usually give specific examples of their contributions to support their assertions.

4. An evaluator from outside the team can conduct performance evaluations by confidential interviews with individual team members. In this scenario, team members one at a time meet with the evaluator to discuss not only their own work but that of others. After talking to all members, the evaluator has a well-developed picture of who did what on the team.

Beyond formal evaluation procedures, the company must develop mechanisms for frequent feedback for its teams. Who will deliver timely praise or blame to the team, and on what evidence? To whom should the team turn for advice and guidance? And how are these sources of feedback linked to the formal performance evaluation system? This last question is particularly crucial.

Some companies have resolved the feedback dilemma by having teams report regularly on their work to an executive or top management committee, one member of which is involved with formal performance evaluation. This is a "no surprises" system of evaluation. Teams know week by week how their work is being received by company officials.

COMPENSATING AND REWARDING

One of the seminal articles in the literature of compensation management is entitled "On the Folly of Expecting A While Rewarding B," by former Academy of Management president Steve Kerr. His point is at once simple and profound: companies cannot hope to direct work behaviors in one direction while the compensation system directs them in another direction.

Take, for example, the recent case of a Silicon Valley chip manufacturer. Top management expected the company's computer technicians to keep up with the latest information in their field by taking after-hours courses offered by area colleges and universities. Management regularly passed out schedules of these classes and made speeches at company meetings about the importance of continuing education. E-mail messages from management to employees nagged them about getting signed up for courses. In short, the company did everything to encourage continuing education for its technicians except to reward them for it.

What kinds of rewards could have motivated employees to stay at the forefront of their field through additional classwork? The employees themselves in this case provided the answer when management wisely decided to pass out a questionnaire. This survey asked workers to give reasons for the poor turnout from the company for continuing education. The compiled responses virtually shouted the answer: we don't attend after-work classes because the company doesn't pay us to do so and doesn't consider this attendance in promotion decisions.

This is increasing the process by which rewards are distributed at Bull HN Information Systems. Executive David Dotlich says that "your ability to work in teams, to get things done through people, and to build teams, is a critical criterion around which we are now ranking people."

The principle at hand seems obvious: we get what we reward. But the reality is that many companies involved in team-based work still compensate according to performance objectives more appropriate for individuals working alone than team members working together. The same standard forms are filled out by managers and signed off by individual team members, even though these forms specify behaviors that have little to do with effective participation on a team.

The prescription to resolve this problem is equally obvious: list behaviors you want to encourage and redesign the compensation plan accordingly to reward those behaviors. Companies who have done so end up with highly motivating ways of paying their workers, including four of the newer approaches to compensation for teams.

Gainsharing

Some companies calculate revenue, profit, or market share gains attributable to a team's work and pay each team member a portion of that gain. In one variation on this theme, the team is given a lump sum payment to be distributed to individual members according to the team's own evaluation of who deserves what.

Bonuses

Other companies negotiate an agreed-upon bonus (in cash, stock options, benefits, or other forms of payment) that will be awarded to teams that achieve their objectives. Sales organizations have used this approach for decades to motivate sales teams. The bonus in these cases often turns out to be a trip to some vacation destination. By rewarding successful teams in this way, sales organizations stroke professional egos, build team spirit, and give public recognition. Bonuses can also be awarded for team suggestion programs (TSPs) that lead to reduced costs or increased revenues.

"Graduation" Promotions

Companies can also arrange team hierarchies so that successful work on a team at one level qualifies the employee for "graduation" to the next higher level team, with higher compensation, a more prestigious title, and more fulfilling challenges or options for professional development. In this case, employees are motivated primarily by their expectation of future rewards. The process is not unlike the "farm" system of professional baseball. The financial success of the few top levels of players provides a powerful motivation to those farm players trying to break into the big leagues.

Knowledge-Based Compensation

Particularly in companies with a relatively fixed product line and predictable skill sets for teams of workers, compensation can be based on demonstrated knowledge or skill levels. In a garment manufacturing firm, for example, one team might be responsible for rough-cut preparation of fabrics for dresses. The skills necessary for this task justify one rate of pay. Members of the team can qualify for higher pay, however, and membership on another team by learning garment construction and sewing skills. In such companies, considerable human and financial resources are devoted to testing programs by which employees can unequivocally demonstrate their new skills. Substantial resources are also usually devoted to training programs providing avenues for employee advancement.

In another example of knowledge-based pay, Shenandoah Life Insurance Company in Roanoke, Virginia, "now assigns teams of 5 to 15 people to serve all the agents and life insurance accounts in a geographical region. Team members must each perform 17 jobs that in the past were separate including processing applications for policies, rating risks, computing premiums, checking data, and maintaining accounts receivable. For each job that they learn and are able to perform, team members get a raise. The results: pay for the 75 employees on teams has increased an average of 37.6 percent in the last two years, while the rest of Shenandoah Life employees have received average increases of 5 percent."

In essence, companies must move away from the "star system," in which stand-out individuals receive the lion's share of rewards and recognition. Instead, the new reward paradigm must be the team player who works (often behind the scenes) with others to achieve company goals.

SAFETY NETS AND ORGANIZATIONAL SECURITY

Employees taking the risk to cast their professional fates with a team need to know in advance the penalties for failure. They realize that, in spite of their best individual efforts, the team may not achieve its goals. Hence their question: would it be better to play it safe as a traditional worker and opt out of team participation?

Companies answer these concerns by policy statements, management communications and speeches, and actions that allow for the possibility of failure (and the learning that comes from it) as well as a permissible degree of risk in team efforts.

Team members empowered to use their best judgment in decision-making also must be allowed to survive the results of those decisions, good or bad. By analogy, a stock broker can't be directed or encouraged to select growth stocks without also being given an implicit "forgiveness factor" if some of those stocks come to nothing. No one picks all winners, and team members must be reassured that their high-risk efforts are supported by the company's high-tolerance confidence and commitment.

One example of a high-risk, high-reward team is IBM's select Advantis group. This team is known within IBM as the "wild ducks"—those that don't fly in usual patterns and expected directions. The primary mission of this elite team is to locate, evaluate, and oversee the acquisition of companies and technologies that fit IBM's future development goals. Of the many smaller firms acquired through the efforts of Advantis, some have impacted products and profits at IBM in stunningly positive ways. But other companies, in spite of the due diligence of Advantis, have proven to be duds after acquisition. Without the knowledge that IBM supports their failures as well as successes, the "wild ducks" could not take the risks necessary to take advantage of many business opportunities.

If the organization has a culture of "time is money" and approves only traditionally structured work days, the company may want to institutionalize a certain breathing space for creativity, even by policy if necessary. 3M Corporation, for example, requires its product development teams to reserve 15 percent of their hours for "time-off thinking"—time for the kind of musing, speculating, reflecting, and playing that lead to unlikely, but extremely successful creations: Post-it Notes, scrub pads that don't rust, and cellophane tape that doesn't cause lines on photocopies.

INTEGRATION OF TEAMWORK AND TRADITIONAL WORK

Few companies convert their entire workforce to team-based work all at once. More commonly, a few teams are created in the midst of any otherwise traditional work organization. Companies must make sure that these islands of innovation exist comfortably within the workforce, without undue pressure to conform to old standards. New teams in old organizations are particularly vulnerable to three influences.

The Favorite Child

Teams can be introduced with so much fanfare by top management that they are stigmatized and ostracized by non-team workers—jealous siblings, as it were. Management must make clear that the work of the team will be evaluated by the same standards of excellence as the work of other employees. All employees should be helped to understand that teamwork is not the only valid approach to work, and that if they are not on a team they are not necessarily out of fashion or on their way out the door.

The Prodigal Son

Teams can quickly develop reputations as rebels and rule-breakers within the organization. Other employees and managers in the organization may look upon these teams as counter-culture groups at odds with prevailing company mores and standards. Teams themselves can do much to defuse this image by avoiding a cloak-and-dagger atmosphere to their work and presenting work-in-progress reports to broad groups in the company. Management can prevent teams from being seen in a negative light by communicating with the general workforce about the team's activities and successes.

The Untouchables

It often happens in organizations that, once team members are drawn away from their usual positions and installed on the team, they lose valuable connections with their former peers and co-workers. These workers, who in a sense have been left behind when they were not selected for teams, may be wary of sharing information, supportive services, or even having daily contact with the "untouchables" on the team. This unfortunate separation can be avoided if team members take it upon themselves to keep up friendly relations with the work divisions from which they came.

In sum, top management must develop a detailed architecture of where teams and teamwork fit in with the usual business structures of the organization. Everyone in the organization, whether team members or not, should know why teams have been formed, how they work, what they hope to achieve, and how their work will be measured against the traditional performance measurement systems in the company.

Troubleshooters

Part of the planning for teams in an organization is preparing for team problems. Teams inevitably need maintenance support and other interventions by experts who know team processes well. Too often the top managers who have selected the teams also appoint themselves as troubleshooters for the teams. The downside of this approach is two-fold: top management may know little about teams or how to resolve their problems; and, top management may be too imbued with organizational power to work candidly in sensitive team situations.

A troubleshooting team may include an executive or two, but should be primarily comprised of experts in team processes—individuals the team trusts and respects to help with its internal problems.

TEAMS AND THE LEARNING NETWORK

The final preparation for teams in organizations looks more toward what can go right than what can go wrong. Through teams, organizations have a superb opportunity to learn about new ways of increasing motivation, reducing turnover, strengthening co-worker bonds, and dissolving unnecessary power hierarchies. Team members themselves can be the best spokespersons for the positive influences they are experiencing within the team. Management should therefore give team members the chance to speak out—in company newsletters, at company meetings, and in widely distributed team reports—about how work is different on the team and why.

EXTERNAL AND INTERNAL WAYS TO RECOGNIZE TEAM PERFORMANCE

The following fourteen items are no-cost or low-cost ways to motivate teams through recognition.

Externally Directed Team Recognition

1. Compliment the work of the team in a memo to top management.

2. Invite a company leader to attend a team meeting with the purpose of praising the team.

3. Create social occasions where the team is honored informally.

4. Ask a newsletter writer in the company or in your industry to develop an article about the work of the team.

5. Seek out professional speaking opportunities (at conferences, service organizations, or industry interest groups) where your team can present aspects of its processes or work.

6. Speak well of the team as often as possible in as many company forums as possible.

7. Nominate the team for competitions and awards within your industry.

Internally Directed Team Recognition

1. Free the team to establish its own work hours and work sites.

2. Ask the team to mentor a less successful team.

3. Make available to the team new technology or other special resources not generally available in the workplace.

4. Share your own challenges with the team and ask their advice.

5. Take the time to respond in detail to reports and other communications sent from the team.

6. Let team members know why they were chosen for the team and the high expectations top management has for the team's work.

7. If the team has none of its own, develop a catchy, affectionate nickname for the team that can be used as a compliment. At Xerox, for example, one top sales team in the photocopier division is known as the "Assassins."

FINAL THOUGHTS ON TEAMS AND TEAMWORK

The promise of teams and their contributions to the workplace of the late 1990s and beyond is potent and attractive. As discussed in the previous chapters, teams can increase employee commitment to company projects through the encouragement of empowerment; of innovative problem-solving approaches at all levels within the company; and of camaraderie and a "we-can-do-it" spirit among company employees. The organization benefits by higher quality product, increased productivity, heightened sensitivity to customer needs, improved (decentralized) decision-making; and, in general, better use of the latent skills and abilities in the workforce.

Teams are changing the way America works. With proper planning, careful selection of team members, and quick resolution of team problems, teams can revolutionize your workplace as they have GE, Champion International, Ford, Digital Equipment Corporation, Procter & Gamble, Boeing, Xerox, Blue Cross, Motorola, Westinghouse, and hundreds of other companies large and small.

Team-Building Tips

1. Provide training so that traditional workers can develop the skills and abilities necessary for effective team participation.

2. Realign resources, performance evaluations, and compensation policies to suit team-based work.

3. Establish organizational safety nets so that, when team members take reasonable risks, they feel supported and safe—that they aren't endangering their reputations, positions, or compensation levels in the organization.

4. Integrate team experiences into the worklife of the company so that non-team employees can learn what team-based work is all about.

1

Problem-Identification Instruments

Chapter 6 discussed the need to quantify or otherwise measure a problem ("put a number on it") as the first step in developing solutions. The instruments in this appendix are by no means exhaustive, but they are a good sampling of approaches that can be used.

A. FISHBONE (ISHIKAWA) DIAGRAM

Uses: To identify causes of the problem

Background: Cause-effect diagrams are used in brainstorming sessions to examine factors that may influence a given situation. An "effect" is a desirable or undesirable situation, condition, or event produced by a system of "causes."

Step by Step:

1. Explain where you are in the problem-solving process and what you would like to do. You might say, "We agree that broken tables are a serious problem. Let's construct a fishbone diagram to see what the causes are."

2. Draw a basic diagram and ask the group to identify the major causes. Use these causes as labels for each branch.

3. Continue soliciting causes from the group adding them to the diagram where appropriate.

4. Once the group has listed all the causes that come to mind, use other techniques to decide which causes could be eliminated.

Example:

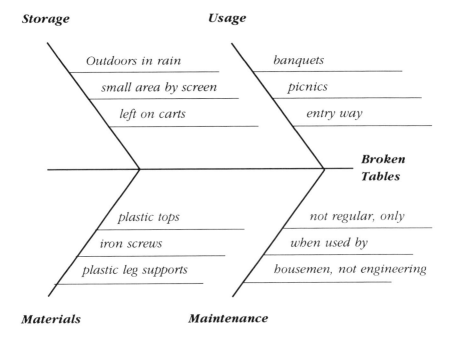

B. PROBLEM-SOLVING: SINGLE LOOP AND DOUBLE LOOP

Many of the problems we encounter every day are simple and easy to solve. For example, if you find a scrap of paper on the floor, you probably just pick it up. That's an example of SINGLE LOOP problem-solving. You see a problem and solve it.

Other problems are more complex. For example, if you find trash on the floor at the same time and place every day for a week, you might get tired of picking it up and ask "Why is this happening?" The minute you asked why, you would have embarked on DOUBLE LOOP problem-solving. In double loop mode, you not only solve the immediate problem. You also try to correct or eliminate the conditions that cause the problem.

The distinction between single and double loop problem-solving is important because they call for different approaches. Teams should concentrate on double loop problem-solving. Here are some examples to help you keep the difference in mind.

The Problem	Single Loop	Double Loop
Employee antagonizes coworkers	Coach Threaten Replace	Selection Promotion Rewards Training
Lost file	Search Replace	File tracking system Duplicate files
Too little time	Work extra hours, evenings, or weekends	Staffing Delegation Priorities

C. Histogram

Uses: To describe the problem in detail; analyze the chain of customers; identify causes of the problem; monitor ongoing performance

Background: A histogram is a bar graph used to display how often different events occur. It is a very effective way to summarize your observations based on check sheets, comment cards, 5 line calls, and other measurements.

Step by Step:

1. Explain where you are in the problem-solving process and what you would like to accomplish. You might say something like, "We have gathered a lot of information. Let's construct a histogram to see what things look like."

2. Cluster your observations together by type and count the number in each category.

3. Select a scale that makes good use of the materials you have without distorting the numbers.

4. Using a pencil, ruler, and straightedge, make a rough draft of the graph.

5. When you are satisfied with your rough draft, use marking pens to make labels, bars, and boundaries more visible.

Example: A sample check sheet showed that 22 guests arrived by car, 14 by limo, 5 by taxi, and 2 another way. Here is what a histogram for the data looks like.

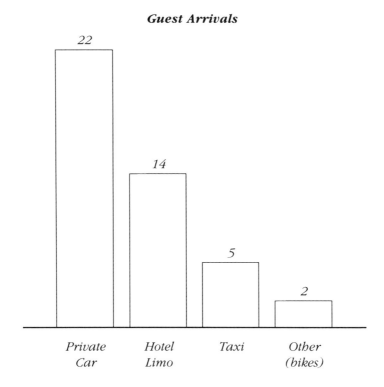

Guest Arrivals

D. PARETO CHART

Uses: To select a problem to study; describe a problem in detail; identify causes of the problem; monitor ongoing performance

Background: The Pareto chart is named for an Italian mathematician who discovered the 80/20 rule. This distribution is important in quality programs because about 20% of situations cause 80% of the problems. The Pareto chart is like a histogram except that it uses percentages instead of raw numbers.

Step by Step:

1. Explain where you are in the problem-solving process and what you would like to accomplish. To identify a problem for study, you might say, "We have looked at lots of comment cards. We may find that many negative comments are caused by just a few situations. Let's construct a Pareto chart to see what the most significant problems are."

2. Gather the data you need to work with.

3. Divide the data into categories.

4. Count the number of items in each category and add them up to get a total.

5. Convert all of the raw numbers to percentages. Divide the number of items in each category by the total.

6. Organize the categories, beginning with the largest percentage and moving to the next smaller until all categories are included in your list.

7. Using a pencil, ruler, and straightedge, draw bars showing the percent of items in each category.

8. When you are satisfied with your chart, use marking pens to make labels and bars easy to read.

Example: Assume that you are reviewing customer comment cards. Most are positive, but 20 make negative comments. Of these, 16 (80%) complain about parking problems, and 1 each complains about 4 other things. Your Pareto chart would look like the one that follows.

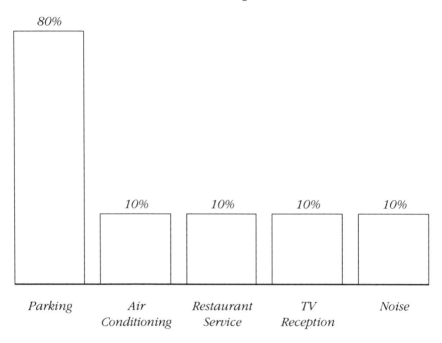

Customer Complaints

Note: Totals exceed 100 percent.

E. Check Sheet (Tally Sheet)

Uses: To describe the problem in detail; analyze the chain of customers; identify causes of the problem; monitor ongoing performance

Background: The purpose of a check sheet is to provide a systematic means for recording information.

Step by Step:

1. Explain where you are in the problem-solving process and what you would like to do. You might say something like, "We have opened up an interesting question. I think we need more information to develop our answer and I think we should try creating a check sheet."

2. Identify the behavior or events you want to count. For example, if you are concerned about how people come to the hotel, your list might include private cars, hotel limo, taxi, and other.

3. Create a form that will make it easy to record your observations.

4. Decide when and where you will observe the behavior or event, and assign people to watch and count.

5. After a count has been made, summarize your data to see if it confirms your suspicions.

6. Report to the group.

Example:

```
                      CHECK SHEET
                     HOTEL ARRIVALS
                       9 am–Noon

         Private Car    ///// ///// ///// ///// //

         Hotel Limo     ///// ///// ////

         Taxi           /////

         Other          //
```

F. HOUSE OF QUALITY

Use: To identify causes of the problem

Background: The house of quality is one of the most sophisticated problem-solving techniques and you probably won't use it very often. However, it is one of the best ways of seeing how different parts of a problem fit together. For example, you might use it to see how an organization or process affects customers. And, you can use it to understand effects on both internal and external customers.

Step by Step:

1. Explain where you are in the problem-solving process and what you would like to do. You might say, "It sounds like the way we're organized affects our customers. Let's construct a house of quality to see if there is a relationship."

2. Identify the qualities that are most important to your customers.

3. List the major characteristics of the organization or system you are studying.

4. Draw the outlines of the house of quality writing in the qualities important to your customers and the characteristics of the organization or system.

5. Lead the group to look at each box formed by the house of quality. In each box, use a ++ to show that the characteristic has a strong positive effect on the quality, a + to show that it has a positive effect, a 0 to show that it is neutral, a – to show that it has a negative effect, and a – – to show that it has a very negative effect.

6. Lead the group to look at the diamonds in the "roof" of the house. Use a ++ to show that the two characteristics have a strong positive effect on each other, a + to show that they have a positive effect on each other, a 0 to show that they are neutral, a – to show that they have a negative effect on each other, and a – – to show that they have a very negative effect.

Example: Assume that you are studying the way the division of labor affects guests arriving at the hotel for the first time. The guests probably want things to go quickly and smoothly, but in most hotels they have to deal with three different people: the doorman, the desk clerk, and a bellhop. The following box shows what a partial house of quality would look like.

Value to Guests	*Greeting by doorman*	*Luggage to bellhop*	*Check by desk clerk*	*Luggage carried by bellhop*	*Guests' experience*
Simple, straight-forward process					
Rapid check-in					
Correct room assignment					

G. CUSTOMER CHAIN ANALYSIS

Use: To analyze the chain of customers

Background: Problems often show up "down the line" from the cause. To avoid overlooking important causes, establish a chain of customers including at least the end user and two supplier steps. Remember, everyone has a customer, either internal or external.

Observed Problem	Supplier Step One	Supplier Step Two	Supplier Step Two
Cu$tomer$ complain about slow seating in the coffee shop	Clean tables are not available to the hostess in a timely fashion	Waitresses experience long delays between placing and receiving orders	Chef lacks critical utensil to prepare some items in a timely fashion

Step by Step:

1. Once the team has identified a problem, you may begin by saying, "Let's look at the chain of customers up to the problem point."

2. Draw a chart like the one above beginning with the observed problem.

3. Ask "Who is closest to the problem?" In our example, it is the hostess.

4. Then ask, "Who supports the person closest to the problem?" and fill in the box.

5. Continue asking "Who supports this person" until you have exhausted everyone in the hotel who is part of the chain.

6. When you have identified the chain of customers, use other techniques to identify problems along the line that could be solved.

H. Run Chart

Uses: To describe the problem in detail; analyze the chain of customers; identify causes of the problem; monitor ongoing performance

Background: A run chart is used to show how things change over time. It is the best way to look for trends. For example, you might use a run chart to see how long it takes guests to check in at different times of the day.

Step by Step:

1. Explain where you are in the problem-solving process and what you would like to do. You might say, "I wonder if things change over time. Let's create a run chart to see what the problem looks like over time."

2. Decide what time periods you will use and how you will measure the problem you are studying.

3. Create a form that will make it easy for one or two people to record their observations.

4. Select the people who will gather data, make copies of the form for them, and make the necessary arrangement.

5. The observers gather the needed data.

6. When the observations are complete, create a rough chart form and record your observations.

7. Before the next meeting, share the chart with other members of the team so they are prepared to review it when you meet again.

Example: You might look at how long it takes a guest to check in between noon and 4 PM. Two members of the team could sit in the lobby and use stopwatches to measure the time it takes each guest to check in. You could use a simple form like this:

Time	Length of Check-In
1 PM	
2 PM	
3 PM	
4 PM	

A chart based on their observations might look like the following.

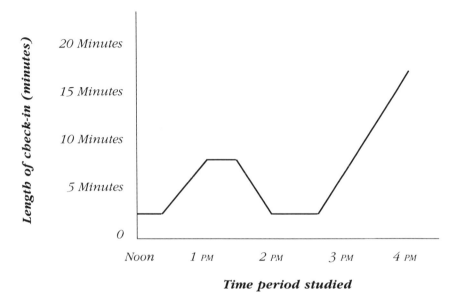

Time period studied

I. SCATTER CHART

Uses: To describe the problem in detail; analyze the chain of customers; identify causes of the problem; monitor ongoing performance

Background: A scatter chart is just like a run chart, except you aren't limited to using time. In fact, you can use a scatter chart to diagram the relationship between any two variables.

Step by Step:

1. Explain where you are in the problem-solving process and what you would like to do. You might say, "We have looked at two aspects of this problem. Let's create a scatter chart to see if there is any relationship between them."

2. Decide how you will measure the two aspects of the problem that interest you.

3. Gather the data you need. Sometimes you will need to use observations. Other times, you will be able to use data that have already been generated.

4. Using a pencil, ruler, and straightedge, create a rough draft of the graph.

5. Plot your data on the graph.

6. When you are satisfied with the rough draft, use marking pens to add labels and make your markings legible.

7. Share the completed graph with members of your team so they will be prepared to discuss it at the next meeting.

Example: Suppose that you are concerned about employees missing work. You think there might be a relationship between age and number of work days missed. You could use a form like this to gather data.

Employee	Age	Days Missed
A	21	8
B	23	7
C	23	9
D	35	4
E	39	5
F	44	3

Notice that this is probably too small a sample to draw any conclusions, but it is good enough for an example. In real life, you would need to look at 20 or more employees before you could draw a reliable conclusion.

A scatter chart based on this data would look like the one below.

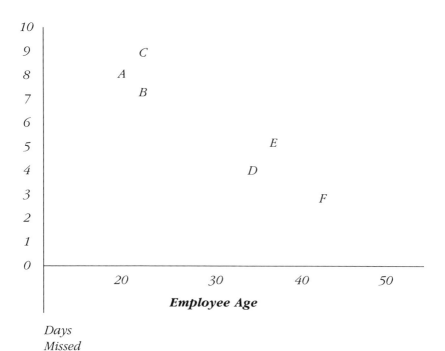

J. Pie Chart

Uses: To describe the problem in detail; to monitor ongoing performance

Background: Pie charts show the relationship between different amounts. For example, you might use a pie chart to show how your group spends its time.

Step by Step:

1. Explain where you are in the problem-solving process and what you would like to do. You might say, "We have talked a lot about how to spend our time as a group. Let's construct a pie chart to show what we're doing."

2. Gather the data you need to construct the chart.

3. Cluster your data into different categories.

4. Count the total number of items in each category and the total number of items.

5. Compute the size of each "slice" of the pie by dividing the number of items in each category and multiplying by 360. Your answer is the number of degrees of the circle for each slice.

6. Draw a circle (your pie) and mark the center point.

7. Draw a vertical line from the center to the top of the circle.

8. Using a pencil, draw a line from the center to the outer edge for each slice. The size of each slice should reflect the number of degrees you calculated in step 5.

9. When you are satisfied with your chart, use marking pens to color the slices and add labels.

Example: Assume that your group has worked together for a total of 25 hours. Of these, 5 hours were spent getting acquainted, 8 hours selecting a problem to study, 4 hours gathering data, 3 hours brainstorming solutions, 3 hours contacting other groups, and 2 hours preparing a briefing. A pie chart showing your efforts would look like this:

Team Time

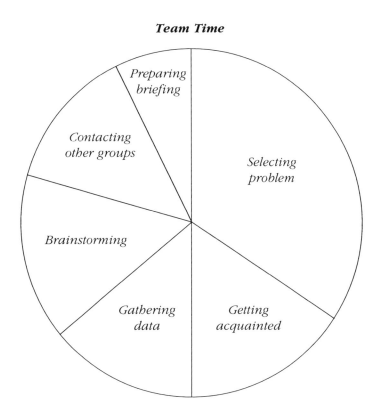

K. WHOM DO YOU SERVE?

This instrument will help teams and team leaders sort out their many obligations and prioritize their work.

Directions: Begin to fill out the following matrix by specifying all those you serve inside and outside the organization. (Include in your concept of service your superiors, subordinates, clients, and others.) For each category of service you specify, fill in the middle columns of the matrix. Consider this evidence carefully as the basis for filling in the "Priority" column with number "1" being the highest priority.

As a team member, I serve:	What I provide:	Benefits		Priority:
		To them:	To company:	

L. Sample Meeting Agenda, with Annotation

Name of Meeting: e.g., Monthly Planning Meeting

Time and Date: Provide a start and *end* time for meeting.

Place:

Attending: Specify those expected to attend the meeting. This will increase attendance.

Primary Purpose of Meeting: This brief statement gives the leader the chance to emphasize the importance of the meeting and focus on main issues.

Agenda Item	Approx. Time	Input	Assignment	Due Date
[Sample]				
1. Acme bid review	15 min.	S. Evans	Counterproposal to Acme—R. Brown	3/9/97

APPENDIX

2

Team Member
Selector

In 1921, the Swiss psychologist Carl Jung proposed the "type" theory of human personality—that is, that each of us is predisposed to certain personality tendencies, which can be described in eight categories:

Member .... vs. .... Self
Thinker .... vs. .... Feeler
Planner .... vs. .... Juggler
Researcher .... vs. .... Closer

Using this model of personality types, business leaders can select team members based on their complementary strengths. Some team members will be more extroverted, some more introverted. Some will spend their energy handling details while others try to grasp the big picture. Some will be predominantly logical in team discussions, while others pay more attention to the emotional impact of the team's work. Some will be skilled data gatherers, while others will tend to draw conclusions and bring closure.

The following diagnostic instrument will help you assess your own personality tendencies in the workplace. If you administer the test to others in your organization, you can determine which of your people will bring complementary skills to their teams.

The Team Member Selector will help you recognize your own predispositions and those of others in regard to the following personality types:

1. The Member (M)   This personality trait predisposes you to enjoy and seek out the company of others in the workplace. The Member joins teams and other groups willingly, looks for ways to include others in activities, and tends to avoid work that must be accomplished alone. The Member relies on consensus decisions in the team and may hesitate to express personal opinions without first having them validated by the group. The Member derives emotional strength from belonging, popularity, and the respect of co-workers.

2. The Self (S)   This personality trait predisposes you to working by yourself. The Self joins teams only for compelling reasons, and even then only for the period of the task at hand. The Self looks with suspicion on widely held opinions and "groupthink." When faced by work tasks too extensive or difficult for a single person to accomplish, the Self opts to divide work into portions that can each be managed by individuals. The Self derives emotional strength from measuring to self-defined standards, not the judgment of others.

3. The Juggler (J)   This personality trait predisposes you to minute-by-minute, seemingly practical adjustments to changing business conditions. The Juggler manages to keep many tasks in progress at once, all in a partial state of completion, with quality of work always a question mark. The panic of impending deadlines and the unpredictability of interruptions and emergencies for the team are all energizing and challenging for the Juggler. It is a matter of pride to the Juggler that he or she can "cope" when others are throwing up their hands in frustration. The Juggler derives emotional strength from a sense of sustained activity as well as a conviction of his or her specialness and value to the team.

4. The Planner (P)   This personality trait predisposes you to place details, individual facts, and other data into patterns. The Planner then clings to these patterns tenaciously, for they serve to organize an otherwise bewildering array of discrete items. The Planner has little tolerance for ambiguity or conflicting information. The Planner tends to resist receiving disorganized data before a plan is in place to handle it efficiently. But after this planning stage, the Planner welcomes information, especially the kind that supports the designated plan. The Planner derives emotional strength from a conviction of his or her usefulness to the team as a shaping, ordering influence.

5. The Thinker (T)   This personality trait predisposes you toward finding, or attempting to find, logical links between thoughts, ideas, concepts, facts, details, and examples. The Thinker insists on postponing action until he or she "figures out" the underlying causes, effects, and relative accuracy or truth of mental propositions and assertions. When in a data-gathering mode, the Thinker is intent on "knowing more"; but when in assimilation and ratiocinating modes, the Thinker may reject or postpone new input of any kind. The Thinker derives emotional strength from the satisfaction of reaching logically defensible solutions to problems. Whether anyone acts on the basis of those solutions is less important to the Thinker than the success of the mental processes involved in arriving at them.

6. The Feeler (F)   This personality trait predisposes you to focus on the emotional content of situations, as experienced personally or by others. The Feeler appraises new information or situations first according to its emotional potential: How do I feel about this? How do others feel? Who will be hurt? Who will be happy? The answers to these questions play a prominent role in shaping the Feeler's eventual point of view and action regarding the new information or situation. The Feeler derives emotional strength from his or her self-image as a sensitive, caring individual and, often, from the friendship of those targeted for his or her empathy.

7. The Closer (C)   This personality trait predisposes you to make conclusions, judgments, and decisions as early as possible during team processes. The Closer is generally impatient with delays urged by others for additional research or planning. The Closer will grant that the whole truth is not known, but argues that enough of the truth is available for decision-making. This personality type can be deaf to input that does not contribute directly to finalizing projects and processes. The Closer derives emotional strength from his or her reputation in the group as an action-oriented, no-nonsense decision-maker and from the satisfaction of having used power and daring to manage difficult problems and personalities.

8. The Researcher (R)   This personality trait predisposes you to postpone judgment and action so long as it is possible to acquire new information. The Researcher craves certainty and suspects conclusions reached without consideration of all the evidence. The

Researcher frequently ignores both time and resource constraints in pressing on with the search for additional data. In communicating that data to others, the Researcher may not be able to successfully organize and summarize the data gathered, since these activities both involve the drawing of tentative conclusions. The Researcher derives emotional strength from the "treasure hunt" excitement of investigation, from the strong influence his or her findings have upon eventual planning, and from the admiration of other team members whose own research skills are less developed.

Directions: Read each question and allow your initial response to guide your answer. In some cases, you may not have a strong preference for either answer. Choose the answer that you agree with most. Do not transfer your choices to the scoresheet at the end of the test until you have completed it.

1. When you walk into a business meeting, do you usually
   a. make conversation with many people?
   b. make conversation with only a few people?

2. When you learn you will be working on a new project at work, do you prefer
   a. to follow a step-by-step approach?
   b. to grasp the big picture first?

3. Do your co-workers value you most for
   a. what you think?
   b. what you feel?

4. Most important business achievements have been due to
   a. a lot of hard work and a little luck.
   b. a lot of luck and a lot of hard work.

5. In the company do you consider yourself to be
   a. popular with many people?
   b. popular with a few people?

6. In learning about a competing company, would you prefer to hear about
   a. what its employees are doing?
   b. what its employees may be able to do?

7. In meeting visitors to your company, do you form impressions based on
   a. their appearance and actions?
   b. personal chemistry?

8. When shopping, do you select items
   a. carefully?
   b. impulsively?

9. At work do you prefer jobs that
   a. bring you in contact with many people?
   b. bring you in contact with only a few people?

10. In your opinion, is speculation about unidentified flying objects
    a. foolish?
    b. interesting?

11. As a manager of others, would it be most important for you to be
    a. firm?
    b. friendly?

12. In arranging a business deal with long-time clients, would you
    a. make sure all details were spelled out in writing?
    b. allow trivial details to be left to good faith between the parties?

13. Do you consider yourself to have
    a. many close friends?
    b. a few close friends?

14. Do you think corporate leaders should be
    a. informative?
    b. imaginative?

15. When a co-worker confides in you about a personal problem, do you first
    a. try to think of a solution?
    b. feel sympathy?

16. In romantic relationships, should bonds and understandings between the parties be
    a. stated clearly?
    b. left partially unstated?

17. When meeting a new employee, do you
    a. take the initiative in showing friendliness?
    b. wait for signs of friendliness on the new employee's part?

18. Should children be raised to
    a. learn practical skills and behavior as soon as they are ready?
    b. enjoy childhood fun and fantasies as long as possible?

19. In work relationships, is it more dangerous to show
    a. too little emotion?
    b. too much emotion?

20. In taking a test, would you prefer to deal with
    a. questions with definite answers?
    b. questions that are open-ended?

21. Do you find unexpected encounters with previous co-workers who have quit the company
    a. enjoyable?
    b. somewhat uncomfortable?

22. Do you prefer a poem that
    a. has a single clear meaning?
    b. has many possible meanings?

23. In voting for a congressional representative, do you favor
    a. an intelligent, cool-headed candidate?
    b. a passionate and well-intentioned candidate?

24. Do you prefer business meetings that are
    a. carefully planned in advance?
    b. somewhat spontaneous?

25. In going out for a business lunch, would you prefer to eat with
    a. many people?
    b. one or two people?

26. Presidents of companies should be thoroughly
    a. practical.
    b. aware.

27. Would you prefer that business acquaintances passing through your city
    a. make specific arrangements to see you in advance of their trip?
    b. call on the spur of the moment when they arrive?

28. When given a time for arrival at a social gathering, are you
    a. usually right on time?
    b. usually somewhat late?

29. When conducting business conversations on the phone, do you usually
    a. make most of the conversation?
    b. respond in brief comments to what the other person is saying?

30. In general, would you prefer to read
    a. a letter to the editor in a newspaper?
    b. a modern poem?

31. Do you prefer to see movies that
    a. reveal social conditions?
    b. produce tears or laughter?

32. In preparing for a job interview, do you think you should prepare to talk more about
    a. your achievements?
    b. your future plans and goals?

33. If forced to accept dormitory accommodations during a conference, would you prefer to stay in a room
    a. with a few other compatible conference participants?
    b. alone?

34. In general do you act on the basis of
    a. the situation at hand?
    b. your mood?

35. If you were hiring employees to work for you, should they be primarily
    a. intelligent and creative?
    b. loyal and hardworking?

36. In choosing a name for a child, the parents should
    a. decide upon possible names well before the child is born.
    b. wait until the child is born to settle upon the right name.

37. In making a consumer complaint, would you prefer to
    a. call the company?
    b. write the company?

38. When performing an ordinary work task, do you prefer to
    a. do it in a traditional way?
    b. try your own way of doing it?

39. In court, judges should
    a. follow the letter of the law.
    b. use their own discretion in interpreting the law.

40. If you are given a project to complete, would you prefer to turn it in
    a. by a set deadline?
    b. when you feel it is ready to turn in?

41. When introducing two of your friends who do not know each other, do you
    a. tell them each a bit of information about the other?
    b. let them make their own conversation?

42. Which is worse for a manager?
    a. To be too idealistic.
    b. To be too much in a routine?

43. When you listen to a business presentation, do you prefer a speaker
    a. who proves his or her points?
    b. who feels deeply about what he or she is saying?

44. At the end of the business day, do you spend more time thinking about
    a. what you did during the day?
    b. what you will do tomorrow?

45. In planning your ideal vacation, would you choose a place where
    a. you can meet family and friends?
    b. you can be alone or with only one or two friends?

46. Which mental activity appeals more to you?
    a. analysis.
    b. prediction.

47. Which would be more important to you if you were president of a company?
    a. that all employees understood their job responsibilities thoroughly.
    b. that all employees felt part of the company family.

48. If you were a member of a project team, would you prefer to be most active during the
    a. completion stage of the project?
    b. initial conceptualization of the project?

49. In learning a new work-related skill, would you prefer to be taught
    a. as part of a small class?
    b. one-on-one by a tutor?

50. In choosing leisure reading, would you be more likely to choose
    a. a historical novel?
    b. a science fiction novel?

51. In planning your career, should you
    a. plan all career moves well in advance?
    b. go with the flow of opportunity?

52. In a luncheon speech paying tribute to an industry leader, should you focus primarily on the person's
    a. accomplishments?
    b. aspirations?

53. Do you think the primary purpose of meetings in business is
    a. to get to know one another and build team spirit?
    b. to get work done as efficiently as possible?

54. Do you consider yourself as having a good head for
    a. facts?
    b. speculation?

55. The most important quality that employees can have is
    a. individual initiative.
    b. team spirit.

56. As a rule, do you consider yourself
    a. a hard worker?
    b. easygoing?

57. If your employer wanted to honor you at a luncheon, would you prefer that the luncheon be attended by
    a. many company employees?
    b. your employer and only one or two others?

58. In general, which quality has been more valuable in the development of successful companies?
    a. common sense.
    b. inspired insight.

59. What is the best thing that can be said about a retiring employee?
    a. that he or she was excellent at his or her job.
    b. that he or she cared about fellow workers.

60. At the time they become engaged to be married, a couple should
    a. set a definite date for the wedding.
    b. leave the wedding date open for a while.

Transfer your answers as checks in the appropriate spaces below

1a___ b___	2a___ b___	3a___ b___	4a___ b___
5a___ b___	6a___ b___	7a___ b___	8a___ b___
9a___ b___	10a___ b___	11a___ b___	12a___ b___
13a___ b___	14a___ b___	15a___ b___	16a___ b___
17a___ b___	18a___ b___	19a___ b___	20a___ b___
21a___ b___	22a___ b___	23a___ b___	24a___ b___
25a___ b___	26a___ b___	27a___ b___	28a___ b___
29a___ b___	30a___ b___	31a___ b___	32a___ b___
33a___ b___	34a___ b___	35a___ b___	36a___ b___
37a___ b___	38a___ b___	39a___ b___	40a___ b___
41a___ b___	42a___ b___	43a___ b___	44a___ b___
45a___ b___	46a___ b___	47a___ b___	48a___ b___
49a___ b___	50a___ b___	51a___ b___	52a___ b___
53a___ b___	54a___ b___	55a___ b___	56a___ b___
57a___ b___	58a___ b___	59a___ b___	60a___ b___
M S	J P	T F	C R

How to Interpret Your Scores

Your totals on the scoresheet will suggest relative tendencies among the eight possible personality-trait predispositions. The higher the score, the more intense that trait is in your total personality. Based on your scores, you can get an approximate idea of which strengths you bring to the team.

APPENDIX

3

Notes

CHAPTER 1. TEAMS IN CONTEXT

1. Cited in Andrew Leigh and Michael Maynard, *Leading Your Team* (London: Brealey Publishing, 1995), p. 142.

CHAPTER 2. CREATING THE TEAM

1. Cited in Glenn M. Parker, *Team Players and Teamwork* (San Francisco: Jossey-Bass Publishers, 1996), p. 16.
2. Cited in B. Harper and A. Harper, *Succeeding as a Self-Directed Work Team* (New York: MW Publishing, 1994), p. 21.
3. Carl Harshman and Steven Phillips, *Teaming Up* (San Diego: Pfeiffer, 1994), p. xii.
4. Thomas Kuhn, *The Structure of Scientific Revolutions* (Chicago: University of Chicago Press, 1984), p. 23.
5. Cited in Harper, p. 19.
6. Glenn M. Parker, *Cross-Functional Teams* (San Francisco: Jossey-Bass Publishers, 1994), p. 6.
7. Jack Gordon, "Work Teams: How Far Have They Come?," *Training,* October 1992, pp. 59–64.
8. Personal interview conducted May 5, 1995.
9. Cited in Don Martin, *Team Think* (New York: Dutton, 1993), p. 48.

10. Cited in Glenn M. Parker, *Team Players and Teamwork* (San Francisco: Jossey-Bass, 1996), p. 11.
11. Cited in S. Kumar and Y. Gupta, "Cross-Functional Teams Improve Manufacturing at Motorola's Austin Plant," *Industrial Engineering,* May 1991, p. 34.
12. Max DePree, *Leadership Jazz* (New York: Macmillan, 1992), p. 38.
13. Richard Guzzo and Eduardo Salas, *Team Effectiveness and Decision-Making in Organizations* (San Francisco: Jossey-Bass, 1995), p. 214.
14. Guzzo and Salas report the research of B. Walker and W. Hanson, "Valuing Differences at Digital Equipment Corporation," in E. Jackson, ed., *Diversity in the Workplace* (New York: Guilford Press, 1995), p. 120.
15. Personal interview conducted June 1, 1996.
16. Bruce W. Tuckman, "Development Sequence in Small Groups," *Psychological Bulletin,* 1955, 63(6), pp. 384–399.
17. Personal interview conducted May 15, 1996.

CHAPTER 3. LEADING TEAMS

1. Cited in John H. Zenger, et al., *Leading Teams* (Homewood: Irwin, 1994), p. 182.
2. Cited in Don Martin, p. 222.
3. Cited in Andrew Leigh and Michael Maynard, *Leading Your Team,* (London: Brealey Publishing, 1995), p. 9.
4. "Establishing the Credibility Factor," *Best Practice,* January 1994, p. 121.
5. Deborah Harrington-Mackin, *Keeping the Team Going* (New York: American Management Association, 1996), p. 15.
6. Leigh and Maynard, p. 126.

CHAPTER 4. PARTICIPATING ON TEAMS

1. Cited in Don Martin, *Team Think* (New York: Penguin, 1993), p. 188.
2. Cited in Jon R. Katzenbach and Douglas K. Smith, *The Wisdom of Teams* (Boston: Harvard Business School Press), p. 50.
3. Katzenbach and Smith, pp. 20–21.
4. Katzenbach and Smith, p. 24.

5. Rensis Likert, *New Patterns of Management* (New York: McGraw-Hill, 1961), pp. 45–48.
6. Richard Wiegand, *Supervisory Management,* July 1986, p. 38.
7. Walter Kiechell III, *Fortune,* May 26, 1986, p. 177.
8. B. Y. Augur, *Supervisory Management,* August 1980, p. 36.
9. Adapted from A. Bell, *Mastering the Meeting Maze* (Reading: Addison-Wesley, 1990), pp. 70–71.

CHAPTER 5. USING TEAMS EFFECTIVELY

1. Jon R. Katzenbach and Douglas K. Smith, *The Wisdom of Teams* (Boston: Harvard Business School Press, 1993), p. 18.
2. *New York Times,* August 7, 1994, C4.
3. Tom Peters, "Service with Soul" (video recording, 1995), and Russell Teasley and Richard Robinson, "Southwest Airlines," cited in John A. Pearce II and Richard B. Robinson Jr., *Strategic Management,* 5th edition (Homewood: Irwin, 1994), p. 84.
4. Tim Keenan, "Young Lions Roar: A.O. Smith Barrio Team Practices Cutting-Edge Management," *Ward's Auto World,* May 1995, p. 73+.
5. Mary G. Rendini, "Team Effort at Maguire Group Leads to Ethics Policy," *HR Magazine,* April 1995, p. 63+.
6. John L. Morris, "Bonus Dollars for Team Players," *HR Magazine,* February 1995, p. 76+.
7. John Nirenberg, "From Team Building to Community Building," *National Productivity Review,* Winter 1994, vol. 14, no. 1, p. 51+.
8. Dee Hope, "Cintas Carves Custom Niche: High-Tech Investment and a Team-Based Corporate Culture Allow This Uniform Maker to Process 60,000 Customized Garments Per Day," *Apparel Industry Magazine,* December 1994, p. 14+.

CHAPTER 6. PROBLEM-SOLVING WITH TEAMS

1. Cited in John H. Zenger, et al., *Leading Teams* (Homewood: Irwin, 1994), p. 270.
2. Commercial versions of the MBTI are available to certified users from the Consulting Psychologists Press, 3803 East Bayshore Road, Palo Alto, CA 94303, tel. (415) 969-8901. A general introduction and abbreviated version of the instrument are published in David Keirsey and Marilyn Bates, *Please Understand Me* (Del Mar:

Prometheus Nemesis Book Company, 1984), while the best general introduction is Isabel Briggs Myers and Mary H. McCaulley, *Manual: A Guide to the Development and Use of the Myers-Briggs Type Indicator* (Palo Alto: Consulting Psychologists Press, Inc., 1985).

CHAPTER 7. TROUBLE-SHOOTING TEAM OBSTACLES

1. Cited in Don Martin, *Team Think* (New York: Penguin, 1993), p. 9.
2. Personal interview conducted February 5, 1996.
3. Cited in Martin, p. 48.
4. Leigh and Maynard, p. 143.
5. Glenn M. Parker, "Leadership Insights," *Today's Team Facilitator,* September 1993, p. 8.

CHAPTER 8. TECHNOLOGY FOR TEAMWORK

1. Don Mankin, Susan G. Cohen and Tora K. Bikson, *Teams and Technology* (Boston: Harvard Business School Press, 1996), p. 14.

CHAPTER 9. SUPPORTING THE TEAM

1. Jack Gordon, "The Team Troubles that Won't Go Away," *Training Magazine,* August 1994, p. 31.
2. Cited in Katzenbach, p. 17.
3. Quoted in Harper, p. 25.
4. J. McClenahen, "Not Fun in the Sun," *Industry Week,* October 15, 1990, p. 23.
5. C. O'Dell, "Team Play, Team Pay—New Ways of Keeping Score," *Across the Board,* November 1989, p. 44.

Suggested Readings

With interest continuing in teams and teambuilding, new literature is appearing every day. The following pages organized into 7 categories list some of the more interesting readings you may wish to consult.

1. Building teams

2. Creativity and problem solving

3. Group practices

4. Leadership

5. Recent innovations

6. Strategic perspectives

7. Team compensation

BUILDING TEAMS

———— "Is It Really a Team?" *Managers Magazine,* January 1995 v70 n 1 p23(3).

Abelson, M. A., & Woodson, R. W. "Reviews of Research on Team Effectiveness: Implications for Teams in Schools," *School Psychology Review,* (1983). 12, 125–136.

Armour, Norton L., "The Beginning of Stress Reduction: Creating a Code for How Team Members Treat Each Other," *Public Personnel Management,* Summer 1995 v24 n2 p127(6).

Brown, Tom, "Teams Can Work Great . . . But Forging a Team Takes a Great Deal of Work!" *Industry Week,* February 17, 1992 v241 n4 p18(1).

Buck, J. Thomas, "The Rocky Road to Team-Based Management," *Training & Development,* April 1995 v49 n4 p35(3).

Burns, Greg, "The Secrets of Team Facilitation," *Training & Development,* June 1995 v49 n6 p46(7).

Carbone, Loret, "How to Build a Winning Team," *Restaurant Hospitality,* February 1995 v79 n2 p34(1).

Cox, Allan, "The Homework Behind Teamwork: Creating a Winning Team Is a Process That Is Dependent Upon a Set of Seven Core," *Industry Week,* January 7, 1991 v240 n 1 p21(3).

Dyer, J. L., "Team Research and Team Training: A State-of-the-Art Review," In F. A. Muckler (Ed.), *Human Factors Review* (pp. 285–323). Santa Monica, CA: Human Factors Society 1984.

Fryberger, Sarah J., "Team Building" *Meetings & Conventions,* May 1995 v30 n6 p118(3).

Gruner, Stephanie, "The Team-Building Peer Review," *Inc.,* July 1995 v17 n 10 p63(3).

Kezsbom, Deborah S., "Making a Team Work: Techniques for Building Successful Cross-Functional Teams," *Industrial Engineering,* January 1995 v27 n 1 p39(3).

Lyman, Dilworth; Richter, Ken, "QFD and Personality Type: The Key to Team Energy and Effectiveness," *Industrial Engineering,* February 1995 v27 n2 p57(4).

Mitchell, R. "Team Building by Disclosure of Internal Frames of Reference," *Journal of Applied Behavioral Science* 22 (1986): 15–28.

Nirenberg, John, "From Team Building to Community Building," *National Productivity Review,* Winter 1994 v14 n 1 p51(12).

Rentsche, Joan R.; Heffner, Tonia S.; Duffy, Lorraine T., "What You Know Is What You Get from Experience: Team Related to Teamwork Schemas," *Group & Organization Management,* December 1994 v19 n4 p450(25).

Stockwell, Amy C., "The Right Way to Team with Suppliers," *Food & Beverage Marketing,* June 1995 v14 n6 p30(2).

Temme, Jim; Katzel, Jeanine, "Calling a Team a Team Doesn't Mean That It Is: Successful Teamwork Must Be a Way of Life," *Plant Engineering,* January 9, 1995 v49 n 1 p112(2).

Tompkins, James A., "The Genesis Enterprise, Part Three: The New, Team-Based Organization," *Modern Materials Handling,* May 1995 v50 n6 p32(1).

CREATIVITY AND PROBLEM SOLVING

Adams, James L., *The Care & Feeding of Ideas.* Reading, Mass.: Addison-Wesley Publishing Company, Inc., 1986.

Buzan, Tony. *Use Both Sides of Your Brain.* 3rd. ed.; New York: Penguin Books, USA Inc., 1989.

Coleman, Daniel, *et al. The Creative Spirit.* New York: Penguin Books USA Inc., 1992.

de Bono, Edward. *Serious Creativity.* New York: HarperBusiness, 1992.

Drucker, Peter F. *Innovation and Entrepreneurship.* New York: Harper & Row, Publishers, 1986.

Hare, A. Paul. *Creativity in Small Groups.* Beverly Hills: Sage Publications, 1982.

Harman, Willis, and Howard Rheingold. *Higher Creativity.* Los Angeles: Jeremy P. Tarcher, Inc., 1984.

Mitroff, Ian. *Break-Away Thinking.* New York: John Wiley & Sons, 1988.

Nadler, Gerald, and Shozo Hibino. *Breakthrough Thinking.* Rocklin, CA: Prima Publishing & Communications, 1990.

Osborn, Alex F. *Applied Imagination.* 3rd revised edition; New York: Charles Scribner's Sons, 1979.

Ray, Michael, and Rochelle Myers. *Creativity in Business.* Garden City New York: Doubleday & Company, Inc. 1986.

Shapiro, Eileen C. *How Corporate Truths Become Competitive Traps.* New York: John Wiley & Sons, Inc., 1991.

Von Oech, Roger. *A Whack on the Side of the Head.* New York: Warner Books, Inc., 1983.

———— "Managing Change: How to Lead a Corporate Revolution," *Fortune,* November 28, 1994.

———— "Managing in the Era of Change," *Fortune,* December 13, 1994.

Barry, David, "Managing the Bossless Team: Lessons in Distributed Leadership," *Organizational Dynamics,* Summer 1991, pp. 31–47.

Blumenthal, Barbara and Philippe Haspeslaugh, "Opinion: Toward a Definition of Corporate Transformation," *Sloan Management Review,* Spring 1994.

Bolman, Lee G. and Terrence E. Deal, "What Makes a Team Work?" *Organizational Dynamics,* Autumn 1992, pp. 34–44.

Fisher, K. Kim, "Managing in the High-Commitment Workplace," *Organizational Dynamics,* Winter 1989, pp. 31–50.

Hackman, Richard and Richard E. "Leading Groups in Organizations," in P. S. Goodman & Associates (Eds.), *Designing Effective Work Groups.* San Francisco, CA: Jossey-Bass, 1986, pp. 72–119.

Hambrick, Donald C., "The Top Management Team: Key to Strategic Success," *California Management Review,* 30 (Fall 1987), pp. 88–108.

Hirschhorn, Larry. *Managing in the New Team Environment.* Reading, MA: Addison-Wesley, 1991.

Kotter, John P., "Leading Change: Why Transformation Efforts Fail," *Harvard Business Review,* March–April 1995.

GROUP PRACTICES

Arthur, Mike, "Rover Managers Learn to Take a Back Seat," *Personnel Management,* October 1994 v26 n 10 p58(4).

Bantel, Karen A., "Strategic Planning Openness: The Role of Top Team Demography," *Group & Organization Management,* December 1994 v19 n4 p406(19).

Bettenhausen, K. L., "Five Years of Groups Research: What We Have Learned and What Needs to Be Addressed," *Journal of Management,* 17, (1991) 345–381.

Fisher, Marshall L., Janice H. Hammond, et al., "How the Right Measures Help Teams Excel," *Harvard Business Review,* May–June 1994, 95–104.

Hackman, J. Richard (Ed.), *Groups That Work (And Those That Don't).* San Francisco, CA: Jossey-Bass, 1990.

Hope, Dee, "Cintas Carves Custom Niche: High-Tech Investments and a Team-Based Corporate Culture Allow This Uniform Maker to Process 60,000 Customized Garments Per Day," *Apparel Industry Magazine,* December 1994 v55 n12 pS14(3).

Isabella, Lynne A.; Waddock, Sandra A., "Top Management Team Certainty: Environmental Assessments, Teamwork, and Performance Implications," *Journal of Management,* Winter 1994 v20 n4 p835(24).

Janis, Irving L. *Group Think.* 2nd ed, revised; Boston: Houghton Mifflin Company, 1983.

Katzenbach, Jon R. and Douglas K. Smith. *The Wisdom of Teams: Creating the High-Performance Organization.* Boston: Harvard Business School Press, 1993.

Kempfer, Lisa, "Building a [Concurrent Engineering] Team," *Industry Week,* July 19, 1993 v242 n14 pC4(3).

Lawler, Edward E., III, *The Ultimate Advantage: Creating the High-Involvement Organization.* San Francisco: Jossey-Bass, 1992.

Miner, F.C., Jr., "Group versus Individual Decision Making: An Investigation of Performance Measures, Decision Strategies, and Process Losses/Gains," *Organizational Behavior and Human Performance,* February 1984, pp. 112–124.

Orsburn, Jack D., *et. al., Self-Directed Work Teams.* Homewood, IL: Business One Irwin, 1990.

Pacanowsky, Michael, "Team Tools for Wicked Problems," *Organizational Dynamics,* Winter 1995 v23 n3 p36(16).

Payne, R., "The Effectiveness of Research Teams: A Review," in M. A. West & J. L. Farr (Eds.), *Innovation and Creativity at Work,* New York: Wiley (1990), pp. 101–122.

Schweiger, D.M. & Sandberg, W. R., "The Utilization of Individual Capabilities in Group Approaches to Strategic Decision Making," *Strategic Management Journal,* 10: (1989) 31–43.

Schweiger, D.M., Sandberg, W.R. & Ragan, J.W., "Group Approaches for Improving Strategic Decision Making: A Comparative Analysis of Dialectical Inquiry, Devil's Advocacy, and Consensus," *Academy of Management Journal,* 29 (1986), pp. 51–71.

Schweiger, D.M., Sandberg, W.R. & Rechner, P.L. "Experimental Effects of Dialectical Inquiry, Devil's Advocacy, and Consensus Approaches to Strategic Decision Making," *Academy of Management Journal,* (1989) 32(4): 745–772.

Seers, Anson; Petty, M.M.; Cashman, James F. "Team-Member Exchange Under Team and Traditional Management: A Naturally Occurring Quasi-Experiment," *Group & Organization Management,* March 1995 v20 n 1 p18(21).

Sherer, Jill L. "Tapping into Teams," *Hospitals & Health Networks,* July 5, 1995 v69 n13 p32(5).

Sirkin, Harold, and George Stalk, Jr. "Fix the Process, Not the Problem." *Harvard Business Review,* July–August, 1992.

Sundstrom, E., DeMeuse, K. P., & Futrell, D. "Work Teams: Applications and Effectiveness." *American Psychologist,* 45, (1990). 120-133.

Thomas, J.B. & McDaniel, R.R., "Interpreting Strategic Issues: Effects of Strategy and the Information-Processing Structure of Top Management Teams," *Academy of Management Journal,* 33 (1990), pp. 286–307.

Tully, Shawn, "What Team Leaders Need to Know," *Fortune,* February 20, 1995 v131 n3 p93(4).

Watkins, Edward, "How Ritz-Carlton Won the Baldrige Award." *Lodging Hospitality,* November, 1991.

Welter, Therese R., "An NCR Team That Could: Little Time and Tough Requirements? No Problem," *Industry Week,* June 17, 1991 v240 n12 D48(2).

Wetlaufer, Suzy. "The Team That Wasn't," *Harvard Business Review,* November–December 1994, 22–39.

LEADERSHIP

Manz, Charles C., David E. Keating, and Anne Donnellon, "Preparing for an Organizational Change to Employee Self-Management: The Managerial Transition," *Organizational Dynamics,* Autumn 1990, pp. 15–26.

Steckler, Nicole, and Fondas, Nanette, "Building Team Leader Effectiveness: A Diagnostic Tool," *Organizational Dynamics,* Winter 1995 v23 n3 p20(16).

Verespej, Michael A., "When You Put the Team in Charge." *Industry Week,* December 3, 1990 v239 n23 p30(3).

RECENT INNOVATIONS

———— "How the Internet Will Change the Way You Do Business," *Business Week,* November 14, 1994.

———— "Rethinking Work," *Business Week,* October 17, 1994.

———— "Special Report: Cyberspace," *Business Week,* February 27, 1995. 12.

Anderson, Shannon. "A Framework for Assessing Cost Management System Changes: The Case of Activity Based Costing . . .," *Journal of Management Accounting Research,* v7, Fall 1995, pl (5 1p).

Argyris, Chris, and Kaplan, Robert, "Implementing New Knowledge: The Case of Activity Based Costing," *Accounting Horizons,* v8, September 1994, p83(23p).

Bridges, William, "The End of the Job," *Fortune,* September 19, 1994.

Davis, Stan, and Bill Davidson, *20 20 Vision.* New York: Simon & Schuster, 1991.

Garvin, David A., "Building a Learning Organization," *Harvard Business Review,* July–August 1993.

Hall, Gene, *et al.,* "How to Make Reengineering Really Work," *Harvard Business Review,* November–December 1993.

Hammer, Michael, and James Champy, *Reengineering the Corporation* (New York: HarperBusiness, 1993).

Handy, Charles, "Trust and the Virtual Organization," *Harvard Business Review,* May–June 1995.

Housel, Tom, and Valery Kanevsky, "A New Methodology for Business Process Auditing," *Planning Review,* May–June 1995, 31–36.

Mangan, Thomas, "Integrating an Activity-Based Cost System," *Journal of Cost Management,* v8, Winter 1995, p5(9p).

Marshall, Brent, "Activity-Based Costing at Wavin," *Management Accounting,* v73, May 1995, p28(3p).

McCutcheon, David M., *et al.,* "The Customization-Responsiveness Squeeze," *Sloan Management Review,* Winter 1994.

McGroarty, J., and Horngren, Charles, "Functional Costing for Better Teamwork and Decision Support," *Journal of Cost Management,* v6, Winter 1993, p24(13p).

Mitchell, Mike, and Wycherley, Ian, "ABC from First Principles," *Management Accounting,* v72, June 1994, pS2(2p) 13.

Pine, Joseph, II, *et al.,* "Making Mass Customization Work," *Harvard Business Review,* September-October 1993.

Player, R., and Keys, David, "Lessons from the ABM Battlefield: Getting Off to the Right Start," *Journal of Cost Management,* v9, Spring 1995, p26(13p).

Shields, Michael, "An Empirical Analysis of Firms' Implementation Experiences with Activity-Based Costing," *Journal of Management Accounting Research,* v7, Fall 1995, p148(19p).

Swenson, Dan, "The Benefits of Activity-Based Cost Management to the Manufacturing Industry," *Journal of Management Accounting Research,* v7, Fall 1995, p167(14p).

Vargo, John, and Ray Hunt, *Telecommunications in Business.* Chicago: Irwin, 1996.

STRATEGIC PERSPECTIVES

D'Aveni, Richard A. *Hypercompetition.* New York: The Free Press, 1994.

Hamel, Gary and C. K. Prahalad, *Competing for the Future.* Boston: Harvard Business School Press, 1994.

Stalk, George, Jr., and Thomas M. Hout, *Competing Against Time.* New York: The Free Press, 1990.

Thompson, Arthur A., Jr., and A. J. Strickland, III, *Strategic Management.* 9th ed.: Chicago: Irwin, 1996.

TEAM COMPENSATION

Caudron, Shari, "Tie Individual Pay to Team Success," *Personnel Journal,* October 1994 v73 n10 p40(6).

Gibson, Virginia M., "The New Employee Reward System: Linking Compensation to a Company's Performance Is Beginning to Make Sense for More and More Businesses That Recognize the Changing Nature of the Employer-Employee Relationship," *Management Review,* February 1995 v84 n2 p13(6).

McNerney, Donald J., "Compensation Case Study: Rewarding Team Performance and Individual Skillbuilding," *HR Focus,* January 1995 v72 n 1 p 1(3).

Morris, John L., "Bonus Dollars for Team Players," *HR Magazine,* February 1995 v4 n2 p76(6).

Zigon, Jack, "Oil Company Learns to Measure Work-Team Performance," *Personnel Journal,* November 1994 v73 n 11 D46(3).

Index

Absenteeism, 96
Action plans, 82–83
Administrative responsibilities, 120–21
Advice, 94
Advisory. group and committee, 60–61
Agendas, 81–82
Aging workers, 25
Alliant Hospital and Healthcare
    Corporation, 57
Allied Signal Aerospace, 69
American Express, 6
American Stores, 28
Amex Life Assurance, 31
Associated Press, 112
AT&T, 112–13
Attitudes toward leadership tool, 41–42
Audioconferencing, 104
Augur, B.Y., 50
Authority, exceeding, 92

Bell Communications Research, 17
Best Practice magazine, 36
Bikson, Tora K., 101
Blue chip teams, 72–84
    characteristics of, 12–15
Blue Cross, 131
Boeing, 20, 101–2, 131
Bonuses, 125
Bull HN Information Systems, 124
Buy-in, 26
Buzzer, 91

Champion International, 131
Child Magazine, 57
Chrysler, 9
Cintas, 57
Circular pattern, 70–71
Closer personality type, 22
Coalition formation, 78
Cohen, Susan G., 101
Cohesiveness as problem, 63
Comfort level of team, 27, 46
Command-and-control structure, 6
Communication process, 48
Compartmentalization, 10–11
Compensating and rewarding, 19, 123–
    26
Competence of individual, 59–60
Competition and rivalry, 4
Computerizing processes within
    companies, 10
Conagra, 23–24
Concluder role, 23
Concurrent engineering, 8
Conflict within team, 93
Consensus seeking, 27
"Constructive" conformity, 48
Contrarian, 91
Control tool, internal or external , 39–
    41
Corporate successes, 56–57
Creativity and structure, 76–80
Criticism, 94

Croni, Stephen, 1
Cross-functional teams, 5, 121
Cross-training opportunities, 46
Cummins Engine, 20
Customer, 5, 7–8
Cyberconferencing, 106

Davis, Al, 22, 88–89
Decision making, 49, 58-60, 122
Decision matrix for using teams, 68
Delco-Remy, 1
Delegated leadership, 33
Demographics, 25
DePalma Hotel Corp., 31–32
DePalma, Joseph, 32
DePree, Max, 25
Design teams, 8–9
Develomental leadership, 34
"Devil's dozen," 95–97
Digital cash, 113
Digital Equipment Corporation (DEC),
    26, 36, 131
Discounted performance and resistance
    to teamwork, 46
Disruptive members on team, 89–91
Diversity, 4–5, 25, 27, 120
Divided-loyalties team, 92–93
Documentation, 81–83
Do-nothing team, 92
Dotlich, David, 124
Double-loop problem solving, 14
Dow, 9
DowVision, 112
Dysfunctional syndromes, 70–71

Elected leadership, 33
Electronic messaging, 111–12
Eli Lilly, 113
E-mail, 107
Empowerment of team, 5–6, 34, 48
Enforced consensus, 78
Entry variables, 71
Erskine, Robert, 119
Evaluating performance, 79
    management by objectives method,
    122
Executive tips, 42, 52
Expanded personal introductions, 71–73
Expectations and performance of
    members, 13, 48
Explanations, 94

Facilitation skills, 83–84
Favorite child influence, 128

Feedback
    for leadership, 38–42
    for success, 14
Feeler personality type, 22
The Fifth Discipline, 119
Flexibility, 49, 23–24
Forbes, 2
    Annual Report on American Industry,
    2
Ford, 9, 20, 131
Foreign-born worker, 4–5
Forming stage of team development, 27,
    68
Fortune magazine, 50
    Fortune 100 companies, 35
    Fortune 1000 companies, 5, 110
Fox, William, 17

Gainsharing, 124–25
GE Fanuc Automation North America,
    Inc., 56
Geneen, Harold, 38
General Electric (GE), 9, 20, 118–19,
    131
General Mills, 9
General Motors (GM), 1, 9, 69–70
Globalization, 2–3
Goal setting , 19, 47
Gordon, Jack, 117
Government information, 103–4
"Graduation" promotions, 125
Group
    leader, 19
    polarization, 65
Groupthink, 64–65
Groupware, 107–10
Guzzo, Richard, 25–26

Halo effect in hiring, 22
Harrington-Mackin, Deborah, 37
Harshman, Carl, 18
Health indicators for teams, 26–27
Herman Miller, Inc., 25
Hofmeister, John, 69
Holtz, Lou, 87
Horiuchi, Ko, 26
"Hypercompetition," 4

IBM, 23, 127
Identification with team, 12
Immigration patterns, 4–5
Implementer role, 23
Inclusiveness, 24–25
Individual preparation for team work,
    21–26

Industry Week, 5
Influence of members on each other, 47, 49
Innovator role, 23
Inspector role, 23
Institute for Social Research, 46
Integration of teamwork and traditional work, 127–29
Internal corporate networks on Internet, 110–14
Internal facilitator, 81–82
Internet, 102–104
Interpersonal skills, 19
Intranets, 110–14
Introductions, personal, 71–73
IT&T, 38

Janis, Irving, 62
Juggler personality type, 22

Katzenbach, Jon R., 44, 46, 53
Keeping the Team Going, 37
Kerr, Steve, 121
Kiechell, Walter, III, 50
Knight, Bobby, 43
Knowledge-based compensation, 125–26
Kodak, 43–44
Kuhn, Thomas, 18

Lack of conviction, 44–45
Leadership/leadership styles, 19, 31–42
    delegated, 33
    at a distance, 35–36
    feedback for, 38–42
    role of, 47
    support, 49
    team expectations of, 36–42
Leading questions, 92
Learning network and teams, 129–30
Leigh, Andrew, 94–95
Lesher Communications, 57
Likert, Rensis, 46
Linear pattern, 70–71
Linking function, 47
Local area networks (LANS), 107
"Lost on the Moon," 73–75
Lotus Notes, 107, 110
Loyalty, 46

McDonnell Douglas, 113–14
Maguire Group, 57
Management, 2–5, 97–98, 120
    senior, 11
Mankin, Don, 101

Maynard, Michael, 94–95
Meetings, 19, 49–52
    visuals for, 50–51
Merck, Johnson & Johnson, 20
Minority workers, 4–5, 25
Mission, 13
Mistakes, 37–38
Monsanto, 9
Morgan Stanley, 111–12
Motivation through recognition, 130–31
Motorola, 24, 53–54, 131
Mutual aid, 48
Mutual respect, 47
Myers Briggs Personality Type Indicator (MBTI), 72–73

Netscape, 110, 114
Network World, 110
Networked tools, 107
New venture teams, 9
Nolan, Sarah, 31
Norming stage of development, 29, 68
NUMMI auto plant, 69–70

Obstacles, 94–95
"On the Folly of Expecting A While Rewarding B," 123
Online catalogs, 103
Orders, 94
Organizational environment for team use, 66–67
Organizational politics, 35
Organizational resources, 67
Organizational responses to change, 5–11
Organizer role, 23

Paradigm shift, 18
Parker, Glenn M., 20
Parker, Kevin, 112
Participation, 43–52
    guidelines for, 46–49
    reluctance, 44–46
    tool, 51–52
Pay. *See* Compensating and rewarding
PepsiCo, 26
Perceived influence tool, 38–39
Performance
    evaluations and feedback, 77, 123–24
    recognition, 130–31
Performing stage of development, 29, 68
Personal computer (PC) industry, 3–4
Personal style and resistance to teamwork, 45

Personality inventory, 22, 70, 118
  Team Member Selector instrument, 22
Phillips, Steven, 18
Physical tests, 15
Planner personality type, 22
Planning and implementing, 79
Platform team, 9
POST, 110
Praise, 92
Preparation for team approach, 20–26
Primary tension, 62–63
Problem, 76–77
  top level, 97–98
  within team, 62–63
Problem solving, 14, 69–85
  and decision-making strategy, 58–60
  sessions, 15
  tools, 79–81
Procedures, 13
Process
  champion, 83–84
  for successful teams, 71
  problem solving, 75–79
  questions, 34–35
Procter & Gamble, 20, 131
Prodigal son influence, 128
Project
  characteristics, 64
  teams/task forces, 10–11
Promises, 92
Promoter role, 23

Quad Graphics, 17–18
Quality control, 19
Quality improvement measures, 19

Rank Xerox, 1
Realigning resources, 121–22
Reality check/assessment, 27
Recharging team, 75
Recognition, 130-31
Reengineering, 10
Reluctance to join, 44–46
Requests, 94
Researcher personality type, 22
Resources
  on conventional networks, 106–10
  for team, 67
Reward systems. See Compensating and
  rewarding
"Risky shift" phenomenon, 65
Role playing, 15
Roles of members, 23
Runaway team, 92

Safety nets and organizational security,
  126–27
Salas, Eduardo, 25–26
"Savior syndrome," 18
Scope of situation, 59
Secondary tension, 62–63
Selection
  of solution, 78
  of team members, 22
Self personality type, 22
Self-direction as training topic, 120
Senge, Peter, 119
Shared leadership, 27, 33–35
Shenandoah Life Insurance Company,
  126
Shingles, Geoff, 36
Simulation exercises, 73–75
Simultaneous design, 8
Smith (A.O.) Corporation, 56
Smith, Douglas K., 44, 46, 55
Social tension, 62–63
Solution
  for dysfunctional teams, 94
  implementation, 78-78
Southwest Airlines, 56
Specialist role, 23
Sphinx, 88
Storming stage of development, 27–28,
  70
Success stories, 56–57
Sun Microsystems, 25
Supporting the team, 117–32
  atmosphere, 49
  compensating and rewarding, 123–25
  intergregation of teamwork and
    traditional work, 127–29
  learning network, 129–30
  performance evaluations and
    feedback, 122–23
  realigning resources, 121–22
  recognizing team performance, 130–31
  safety nets and organizational
    security, 126–27
  training, 119–21
Survival exercises, 14–15, 73–75

"Talent divorce," 34
Task force, 10–11
Tasks and schedules, 19
Team
  approach to work, 20–26
  characteristics of health/success, 12–
    15, 26–27
  creating, 17–30

Team *(Continued)*
  culture and conditions, 47
  development, stages of, 27–29
  leak, 87–88
  as primary strategy, 1–15
  problems within, 62–64, 93, 95–97
  project characteristics/organizational
    environment, 66–67
  qualities of effective members, 46–49
  solution, 59
  "spirit," 47
  success, 56–57
  suggestion program (TSP), 124
  vs. traditional work, 18–19
  using effectively, 55–68
  vendors/customers as members of,
    24–25
Team building, 14–15
  success, 71–75
  tips, 30, 84–85, 99, 114–15, 131
Team Member Selector instrument, 22
Teaming Up, 18
Teams and Technology, 101
Technical skills, 19
Technological change, 3
Technology for teamwork, 101–115
Telecommunications, 3, 104–6
Teleconferencing, 104–6
Telephone companies, 3
Textconferencing, 105
Thinker personality type, 22
Threats, 92
Today's Team Facilitator magazine, 97
Tolerance for disagreement, 26
"Tossing the ball," 49
Total quality management, 6–7
Totality of job responsibility, 19

Toyota, 69–70
Training, 47, 119–21
Training Magazine, 21, 117
Troubleshooting
  obstacles, 87–99
  team, 129
  the troubleshooters, 97–98
Trust/caring, 19, 48
Tuckman, B.W., 27–29

Untouchables influence, 128–29
"Us against them" attitude, 19

Values/goals, 47
Vernon, G.B., 24
Videoconferencing, 105–6
Virtual information network, 113
Virtual reality, 106
Volume production, 6
Voting, 76, 121

Web server, 110
Welch, Jack, 118
Westinghouse, 9, 131
Whole-enterprise perspectives, 11
Wiegand, Richard, 50
The Wisdom of Teams, 44, 53
Women, 4, 25
Word hog, 90–91
Work in America Institute, 20
Workforce diversity, 4–5, 25, 27, 120
World Wide Web, 102

Xerox, 131

Zisman, Marty, 110

TITLES OF INTEREST IN
BUSINESS AND INTERNATIONAL BUSINESS

GLOBAL MARKETING IMPERATIVE, by Michael Czinkota, Ilkka Ronkainen, and John Tarrant
MARKETING STRATEGIES FOR GROWTH IN UNCERTAIN TIMES, by Allan J. Magraph
INNOVATION: LEADERSHIP STRATEGIES FOR THE COMPETITIVE EDGE, by Thomas D. Kuczmanski
INTERACTIVE MARKETING: THE FUTURE PRESENT, by Edward Forrest and Richard Mizerski
THE SUCCESSFUL MARKETING PLAN, by Roman Hiebing and Scott Cooper
STRATEGIC DATABASE MARKETING, by Rob Jackson and Paul Wang
CUSTOMER BONDING, by Richard Cross and Janet Smith
MANAGING SALES LEADS by Bob Donath, Richard A. Crocker, Carol K. Dixon,
    and James W. Obermayer
AMA MARKETING ENCYCLOPEDIA, by Jeffrey Heilbrun
BETWEEN CULTURES, by H. Ned Seelye and Jacqueline Howell Wasilewski
HOW TO CREATE HIGH-IMPACT BUSINESS PRESENTATIONS, by Joyce Kupsh and Pat Graves
EFFECTIVE BUSINESS DECISION MAKING, by William F. O'Dell
HOW TO GET PEOPLE TO DO THINGS YOUR WAY, by J. Robert Parkinson
HANDBOOK FOR MEMO WRITING, by L. Sue Baugh
HANDBOOK FOR BUSINESS WRITING, by L. Sue Baugh, Maridell Fryar, and David A. Thomas
HANDBOOK FOR PROOFREADING, by Laura Killen Anderson
HANDBOOK FOR TECHNICAL WRITING, James Shelton
HOW TO BE AN EFFECTIVE SPEAKER, by Christina Stuart
FORMAL MEETINGS, by Alice N. Pohl
COMMITTEES AND BOARDS, by Alice N. Pohl
MEETINGS: RULES AND PROCEDURES, by Alice N. Pohl
BIG MEETINGS, BIG RESULTS, by Tom McMahon
HOW TO GET THE MOST OUT OF TRADE SHOWS, by Steve Miller
HOW TO GET THE MOST OUT OF SALES MEETINGS, by James Dance
A BASIC GUIDE TO EXPORTING, by U.S. Department of Commerce
A BASIC GUIDE TO IMPORTING, by U.S. Customs Service
CULTURE CLASH, by Ned Seelye and Alan Seelye-James
DOING BUSINESS IN RUSSIA by ALM Consulting, Frere Chomeley Bischoff;
    and KPMG Peat Marwick
THE INTERNATIONAL BUSINESS BOOK, by Vincent Guy and John Matlock
INTERNATIONAL BUSINESS CULTURE SERIES, by Peggy Kenna and Sondra Lacy
INTERNATIONAL HERALD TRIBUNE: DOING BUSINESS IN TODAY'S WESTERN EUROPE by Alan Tillie
INTERNATIONAL HERALD TRIBUNE: GUIDE TO EUROPE, by Alan Tillier and Roger Beardwood
INTERNATIONAL HERALD TRIBUNE: GUIDE TO BUSINESS TRAVEL IN ASIA, by Robert K. McCabe
DOING BUSINESS WITH CHINA
MARKETING TO CHINA, by Xu Bai-Yi
THE JAPANESE INFLUENCE ON AMERICA, by Boye De Mente
JAPANESE ETIQUETTE & ETHICS IN BUSINESS, by Boye De Mente
CHINESE ETIQUETTE & ETHICS IN BUSINESS, by Boye De Mente
KOREAN ETIQUETTE & ETHICS IN BUSINESS, by Boye De Mente

For further information or a current catalog, write:
NTC Business Books
a division of NTC *Publishing Group*
4255 West Touhy Avenue
Lincolnwood, Illinois 60646–1975